Pack Up Your Troubles

BOOKS IN THE PROTESTANT PULPIT EXCHANGE

Pack Up Your Troubles

Sermons on
How to Trust in God

Maxie Dunnam

PROTESTANT
PULPIT
EXCHANGE

Abingdon Press
Nashville

PACK UP YOUR TROUBLES:
SERMONS ON HOW TO TRUST IN GOD

Copyright © 1993 Abingdon Press

All rights reserved.

93 94 95 96 97 98 99 00 01 02 — 10 9 8 7 6 5 4 3 2 1

This book is printed on recycled, acid-free paper.

Library of Congress Cataloging-in-Publication Data

Dunnam, Maxie D.
    Pack up your troubles: sermons on how to trust God / Maxie Dunnam.
      p. cm.—(Protestant pulpit exchange)
    Includes bibliographical references.
    ISBN 0-687-09755-X (acid-free paper)
    1. Bible N.T. James—Sermons. 2. Methodist Church—Sermons.
    3. Sermons, American. I. Title II. Series.
    BS2785.4.D86   1993.
    252'.076—dc20   92-42037

The story of Mama Hale in Chapter 8 is excerpted with permission from "Mama Hale and Her Little Angels" by Claire Safran, *Reader's Digest,* September 1984. Copyright © 1984 by the Reader's Digest Assn., Inc.

MANUFACTURED IN THE UNITED STATES OF AMERICA

To three persons

—

Mary Evelyn Marino
Robbie McQuiston
Mary Hall

—

without whose faithful assistance
I could not have been effective in
ministry during the past twenty years.
They served not only as my secretaries,
but as counselors and encouragers.

Contents

CONTENTS

Introduction

If I were to give a subtitle to the Epistle of James, I would call it "A Manual of Practical Christianity." And isn't that our need? We are always asking that things be made more practical. Speakers are admonished to use the "kiss principle": "Keep it simple, stupid."

There is a sense in which the Epistle of James is a how-to book, and any bookstore has a large section of such books, from *How to Build a Patio* to *How to Repair Your Motorcycle*. We are a sort of "do it yourself" people. Many who can afford to have anything and everything done by others like to do it themselves.

The possibility of a how-to manual for the Christian life is appealing. We hear a lot in church about what we should do, but perhaps not enough about how to do it. My prayer is that, throughout this book, I will not forget the "how to," in "How to Trust in God."

I'm aware of the controversy that has surrounded this book of James, even before it was included in the canon of scripture we call the Bible. Unfortunately, Martin Luther tied a millstone around this book's neck when he called it "an Epistle full of straw." He felt there was nothing evangelical about it. I'm aware that there were many pros and cons in its journey to being accepted as a part of Holy Scripture. But the burden of tradition and the church's response to it has given it a place among the General Epistles of the New Testament.

While Luther called it an Epistle of straw, others have called it The Epistle of Rock or Epistle of Reality or Epistle of Common Sense.

So I believe it's a book we are well advised to heed. Its purpose is not to proclaim the life, death, and resurrection of Christ, yet there is wisdom and guidance for those who would be followers of the Risen Lord. In fact, some have even thought it was a commentary on sections of the Sermon on the Mount. Throughout the letter, you will find those words of James, which sound very much like the words of Jesus.

I like to think of it as a manual of discipleship—very practical guidance, as well as challenge and inspiration. Seeing it this way, I preached twelve sermons based on this Epistle to the congregation I serve. I sought to center on the crisp, pungent truths, which fall one after another from the letter.

Some believe that the Epistle was originally a sermon or sermons preached by James, the brother of our Lord, and then recorded in this fashion. In fact, one theory of authorship has it that this was a sermon preached by James in his Aramaic tongue, taken down by someone who translated it into impeccable Greek, edited it, judiciously added to it with loving care, and issued it to the church at large.

So the sermons that follow here center on these pungent points made by James the preacher. I have elaborated on these points and sought to apply them to our lives.

As you read the chapters, stay aware that they are sermons, written to be heard. Few changes have been made from the original text for preaching. My prayer is that in their published form, they may have an added quality that will inspire reflection, questions, and elaboration, to enable readers to apply the message to their lives. In that way, this book will extend the "manual of practical Christianity" dimension of the Epistle of James.

CHAPTER ONE

> *Count it all joy . . . when you meet various trials, for you know that the testing of your faith produces steadfastness. And let steadfastness have its full effect, that you may be perfect and complete, lacking in nothing. (James 1:2-4 RSV)*

Count It All Joy

After a greeting, the Epistle begins with a shout: "Count it all joy!"

No hesitation here. No fumbling to get to the point. No tiptoeing around the thorny issue. And what is the first thorny issue James addresses? Suffering, trials, troubles—all those flies in the ointment, all those thorns in the flesh—all those knockdowns in life—all that being pushed back to the goal line and having to start again. That's where James begins, and he shouts, "Count it all joy!"

Now I can feel you thinking, and maybe saying beneath your breath, "And you call this a how-to book!" To call this an epistle of practical Christianity sounds rather naive. "Count it all joy!" sounds more like a Cloud-9 approach, not a down-to-earth grappling with reality.

Well, at least James gets our attention right off. Anyone who grabs our attention, shoulders and shakes us, looks us straight in the eye, and, with a steady voice, hones in, "Count it all joy!" deserves our hearing. So let's listen to him.

Maybe we will hear best, and appropriate most, if we begin at the end of the verses of our text—the last part of verse 4: "That you may be perfect and complete, lacking in nothing."

That appeals, doesn't it? I mean, isn't that what everybody who wants something from us is offering us—everything? And don't we want it all?

One of my favorite columnists, Russell Baker of *The New York Times*, began a column with these thoughts:

> It's all right to want it all. We have advertisements in praise of wanting it all. "Why settle for less?" they ask. . . . We have television commercials in which people who have it all torment people who don't have it all by making them feel rotten about not having it all. . . . They display their fantastic dental caps, their stunning physiques, their incredible automobiles, their beautiful lodges and oceans and mountains and cities, their ineffably tasty beer, burgers, wine, pizza. "It doesn't get any better than this," they say. Which is another way of saying, "We've got it all."

Accompanying the column is a cartoon of a fellow carrying a placard which reads, "Instant gratification isn't fast enough."

That's an easy trap to fall into, isn't it? We are tempted to want it all, and to want it now.

James demands that we rethink the whole matter of having it all. He suggests we are to be "perfect and complete, lacking in nothing."

But there is a strange twist for our jaded minds and our overindulged appetites. James connects being perfect and complete with suffering. How can that be? "Count it all joy," he says. "Count it all joy when you meet with trials"—and then he closes that admonition by saying, "That you may be perfect and complete, lacking in nothing."

So, what are the lessons here?

The first is elementary, but we tend to forget it. Growth is not easy. Now, that sounds simplistic, doesn't it? How often have you heard it?

This is true of any kind of growth. It isn't easy. It is especially true of Christian growth. That's the reason we have so few truly saintly people. And that's the reason we should be slow to judge the faith and commitment of others. So much of our growth, and so much of the way we express our faith, is dependent upon the kind of people we are—and all of us are different.

There is a story of two Generals during the Civil War. The pressures of battle were intense. One General noticed that the other was visibly afraid.

"Sir," he said, "if I were as frightened as you are, I'd be ashamed to call myself a General in our nation's army."

"Sir," the other man replied, "if you were as frightened as I am, you would have fled the field of battle by now."

None of us knows another person's struggles. We sometimes think we do. But more often than not, what we perceive is far from reality.

It's almost impossible to know what's going on in the depths of a person's life. Our congregation is deliberately seeking to be a place of hospitality for *recovering* persons, folks who know themselves to be addicted to alcohol or other drugs. Sharing with these people has enabled me to feel, at least to a degree, their struggle with control, their low self-esteem, their dependency. Yet, I know I can't begin to plumb the depth of their struggle.

> *"When you are suffering, it doesn't help to compare yourself to others."*

If you followed me around for a few days, you might be surprised by some of my reactions to people, or my feelings of disappointment. If you are not involved with people day in and day out, you may not understand that my reactions and responses are a result of my struggle with pretension, or self-righteousness. I have problems with people who say one thing and mean and do another.

So we need to be careful about judging others. We never know what may be going on inside, driving them to their actions and attitudes. If we are not willing to be patient with people and stick with them until they are free to share their inner struggle with us, we can at least not add to their burden by judging them.

Growth is not easy, and so much of our growth, so much of the way we express our faith, is dependent upon the kind of people we are—and each of us is different.

And that suggests a second truth. When you are suffering, it doesn't help to compare yourself to others.

More than two hundred years ago, a young boy who lived in England was very sick and puny. They didn't have the kinds of medicines back then that we have today. They weren't blessed with the medical technology we know. So he remained in that condition all his life, and never became a physically strong person at all.

When he was young, he would look out the window of his house and watch other children playing in the field. He would become sad as he watched them—at times, even crying—because he wanted to be out there with them, but he couldn't. That made him feel sorry for himself, and jealous and envious of others.

When he was older, he decided that he would go into the ministry, be a pastor of a congregation, and spend his life serving Christ in that way.

But again his health failed, and he was just too frail to carry on his pastoral duties. He became deeply depressed.

"Why can't I be like other people?" he cried out. "They have their health and I don't. They can do things with their lives and I can't. They are out there making a difference, and I'm just sitting here unable to make any difference at all. Why can't I be like them?"

But then one day someone talked with this young man and helped him to see that his life had its own purpose, apart from that of anyone else. He began to realize that he would get nowhere as long as he compared himself with everyone else.

He began to affirm the fact that he had his own life to live, apart from that of anyone else. What mattered was that he live his own life fully and completely, and to the very best of his ability. When he started to do that, he began to change; his life really began to take off.

That man was Isaac Watts, one of the greatest hymn writers of all time. He wrote "Joy to the World" and "O God, Our Help in

Ages Past." His life had no direction, no impelling energy, no creativity, until he stopped looking around, comparing himself with others, and committed himself to living his own unique life.

So, if we are to learn how to "count it all joy," and move through our suffering and trials to be perfect and complete, lacking in nothing, we need to know that it doesn't help to compare ourselves with others.

> *"Pain by itself is evil.*
> *It doesn't teach us anything."*

That pushes us back to a specific word suggested in our text: Suffering can be wasted, or it can produce steadfastness in our faith. That's what James says in verse 3: "For you know that the testing of your faith produces steadfastness."

But pay careful attention to the completion of his thought in verse 4: "For you know that the testing of your faith produces steadfastness, and let steadfastness have its full effect, that you may be perfect and complete, lacking in nothing."

You see, suffering may produce steadfastness and faith, and we still will be incomplete. We still may lack joy. Pain by itself is evil. It doesn't teach us anything. It may discipline us to be strong and not complain. It may turn us into cynics. We may be tough and steadfast in our suffering, always keeping a stiff upper lip, but that's a long way from what James is talking about—"Count it all joy . . . that you may be perfect and complete, lacking in nothing."

Philip Yancey, in *Disappointment with God*, gives us a clue for allowing our steadfast faith in suffering to work its full effect in our life. He tells us about Douglas, who "seemed righteous, in the sense of Job," and who, like Job, suffered terrible afflictions he did not deserve.

Douglas had given up a lucrative career to start an urban ministry. His wife developed breast cancer, had a breast removed, and was struggling with the debilitating side effects of chemotherapy. In the midst of this crisis, a drunken driver hit their car and Douglas sustained a severe brain injury. He suffered terrible headaches and double vision. He could no longer work full-time to support his wife and daughter. He had loved to read, but now struggled to get through a page or two. If anyone had a right to be angry with God, Douglas did.

Philip Yancey expected Douglas to express disappointment with God, but instead, Douglas said that he had learned "not to confuse God with life":

> I feel free to curse the unfairness of life and to vent all my grief and anger. But I believe God feels the same way about that accident— grieved and angry. I don't blame him for what happened. . . . I have learned to see beyond the physical reality of this world to the spiritual reality. We tend to think, "Life should be fair because God is fair." But God is not life. And if I confuse God with the physical reality of life—by expecting constant good health, for example— then I set myself up for a crashing disappointment. . . . We can learn to trust God despite all the unfairness of life. Isn't that really the main point of Job? (pp. 183-84)

Douglas challenged Yancey to "go home and read again the story of Jesus. Was life fair to him? For me, the Cross demolished for all time the basic assumption that life will be fair."

Do you see the difference? It's very clear. We can waste our suffering, or we can allow it to produce trust in God, steadfastness in faith. And we can allow that steadfastness in faith to perfect and complete us—leaving us "lacking in nothing."

So the shout of James is real. "Count it all joy!" And we can do that—if we know that growth is not easy—if we will realize that when we are suffering, it doesn't help us to compare ourselves to others. And, if we will not waste our suffering but allow it to produce steadfastness in faith, that is what will bring us to completion, lacking in nothing.

That's a rather good lesson in practical Christianity, isn't it?

CHAPTER TWO

> *If any of you is lacking in wisdom, ask God,*
> *who gives to all generously and ungrudgingly,*
> *and it will be given you. But ask in faith, never*
> *doubting, for the one who doubts is like a wave*
> *of the sea, driven and tossed by the wind; for the*
> *doubter, being double-minded and unstable in*
> *every way, must not expect to receive anything*
> *from the Lord. (James 1:5-8 NRSV)*

Don't Mess with Mr. In-between

Colin Higgins' novel *Harold and Maude* is fascinatingly different, but warmly convincing. It's the story of two persons who not only affirm each other's existence, but cherish the mutual meanings they share. A young man in his twenties and an enchanting woman in her seventies become real friends. Maude cares for Harold, not because he is useful or ornamental—he is neither. And not because of anything he does or has, but just because he is himself. Harold is thus better able, when he is with Maude, to understand himself and to verbalize his many problems.

One of those problems is an obsession with repeatedly faking his self-destruction. Convincingly, dramatically, and in the most gruesome ways, he has faked suicide again and again. In the presence of Maude, he is able both to understand and to verbalize how he got to this point.

His mother, as far as he was concerned, never had time for him. He felt, quite literally, that she had no regard, much less affection, for him. Then one day something happened. He tells Maude about it in these words:

> "When I got [home], my mother was giving a party, so I crept up the back stairs to my room. Then there was a ring at the front door. It was the police. I leaned over the banister and heard them tell my mother that I had died in an accident at school. I couldn't see her face, but she looked at the people around her and began to stagger."
>
> Speaking very slowly and softly, Harold continued, tears welling in his eyes.
>
> "She put one hand to her forehead. With the other she reached out, as if groping for support. Two men rushed to her side, and then—with a long, slow sigh—she collapsed in their arms."
>
> Harold stopped for a long pause.
>
> "I decided then," he said solemnly, "I enjoyed being dead."
>
> Maude said nothing for a moment. Then she spoke quietly.
>
> "Yes, I understand. A lot of people enjoy playing dead, but they're not dead, really. They're just backing away from life. They're players, but they think life is a practice game and they'll save themselves for later. So they sit on the bench, and the only championship they'll ever see goes on before them. The clock ticks away the quarters. At any moment they can join in."

Maude is right, and that's what James is talking about in our scripture lesson. The captivating image in the text is that of "the double-minded," the doubters. In the language of Maude, such folks are not dead, though they seek to relate to life as though they were. They are not dead, but they back away from life. They treat daily living as a practice game, saving themselves for what they think is the real thing, which will come later.

But let's not get ahead of ourselves. We need to look at the entire lesson, though we will center on this image of being double-minded.

I suggested in the introduction that this Epistle may have begun as a sermon, or sermons. I believe it was more than one sermon. There is too much here. For sure, the letter is not integrated in a structural sense. It is as though the writer is responding out of impulse and emotion, rather than establishing a logical train of thought.

In verses 2, 3, and 4, James talked about suffering and how we are to be joyful in suffering. Now in verse 5, he talks about wisdom. In talking about wisdom, he is talking about being God-centered and single-minded.

We can see wisdom, even feel wisdom, better than we can define it. When you describe a person as *wise*, you know what you mean, but you would be hard-put to define what it is that makes that person wise. We know when we have acted wisely. We feel it, even though we may not be able to give reasons for our action.

When pressed, most of us would agree that wisdom is not philosophical speculation or intellectual knowledge. It is more practical than that. Wisdom is about life, about living rightly. In *The Communicator's Commentary*, Paul Cedars says,

> There is a quality of the wisdom of men which comes primarily from the experiences of life. For example, a person shows wisdom when he or she does not touch a hot stove. Most of us have gained that little bit of wisdom through the painful experience of touching a hot stove at some time in our lives and gaining the desire never to do it again. That is the process of gaining earthly wisdom. Of course, the longer we live, the more "hot stove" experiences we encounter; older people are usually wiser people. James is inviting us, however, to employ a quality of wisdom that far exceeds the earthly kind of wisdom. (vol. 11, p. 27)

Such wisdom has to do with *guidance*, with living life in the way God designed it to be lived. It has to do with knowing who we are as God's children and acting in that fashion.

Norman Neaves, pastor of Church of the Servant in Oklahoma City, tells about Dr. Hendrik Kramer, a missionary in Indonesia for some twenty-three years. Nearly fifty years ago, when he returned home to Holland, the Nazis were overrunning his country and arresting Jews who lived there. They were also arresting many Christians who had resisted Hitler's maneuvers in their homeland.

As conditions grew worse, these Christians began to rely on Kramer for strength and inspiration. He became a pastor to them. Late one night, some of them slipped into Kramer's house and said, "Tell us what to do, Herr Doctor. Our Jewish neighbors are being dragged out of their homes and off to the gas chambers. And many of our own are hearing the knock of the Gestapo on the doors at night. Tell us, Herr Doctor, tell us what to do."

Kramer was silent for a long, long time. Then he spoke with the transparent honesty and conviction that characterized his life and had drawn them to him initially: "I cannot tell you what to do, but I can tell you who you are!" And with that, he picked up his Bible, opened it, and began to read.

That's the wisdom James is talking about—knowing who we are as God's children and living life as God designed it.

Commenting on that story, Neaves said, "We are a peculiar people who live in the midst of the world, those of us who dare to name ourselves after Christ. We might not have all the answers to life's vexing questions. And indeed we don't. But even still, we choose to live by faith."

> *"We can't believe that wisdom is ours for the asking."*

That's the wisdom James is talking about. Specifically now, we ask, How do we get it? We ask for it. That's what James says in verse 5: "If any of you is lacking in wisdom, ask God, who gives to all generously and ungrudgingly, and it will be given you."

There are two hindrances to receiving wisdom. One is our failure to recognize our need. You see that in the text: "If any of you is lacking in wisdom," James says. Our asking is predicated upon recognizing our need for wisdom. We simply will not ask if we do not realize that we have the need.

The second hindrance to receiving wisdom is what I call *the barrier of the simple.* We can't believe that wisdom is ours for the asking. Behind that disbelief is a deeper failing on our part of which we probably are not aware. It is a failure to trust God for who God really is. Look at the way James describes God in verse 5: God gives "to all generously and ungrudgingly."

As we study the Word of God, it is obvious that God delights in giving and that love is the motive for giving: "God so loved the world that he gave his only Son" (John 3:16 NRSV).

The reason we do not receive wisdom, the reason we don't receive the guidance we need, is that we don't ask in faith. It's too simple! It's too good to be true! That's the reason James warns us to ask without doubting."

And that brings us to the image of the double-minded, and our primary focus: "Don't Mess with Mr. In-between." Some of you remember the lines from a song that encouraged us to "accentuate the positive" and "eliminate the negative," but especially cautioned, "Don't mess with Mr. In-between."

However, the message goes further back than that, and it's more than a good upbeat philosophy set to music. It's theology. It's biblical faith. A long time before that popular song, a singer of Israel discerned God saying, "I hate men who are half and half." Then in the closing book of the Bible, John's Revelation, he was instructed to write to the church in Laodicea: "I know your works; you are neither cold nor hot. I wish that you were either cold or hot. So, because you are lukewarm, and neither cold nor hot, I am about to spit you out of my mouth" (Rev. 3:15-16 NRSV).

James says the same thing in our scripture lesson: "For the one who doubts is like a wave of the sea, driven and tossed by the wind; for the doubter, being double-minded and unstable in every way, must not expect to receive anything from the Lord" (6b-8).

As I was preparing for this sermon, I came across a poem about the centipede:

> The centipede was happy quite,
> Until the toad in fun
> said, "Pray, which leg comes first after which,
> when you begin to run?"

This racked his mind to such a pitch,
He lay distracted in the ditch,
not knowing how to run.

Can you identify with the centipede? I can. In fact, we may call it
the centipede syndrome: Being immobilized by so many choices
that we aren't able to make up our minds.

Now, we could preach to the centipede and tell it to do what
comes naturally. That's what it had been doing all along until
the toad confused it. Try to get into the mind of the centipede.
Can you feel its utter confusion? Which of its 50 or 100 or however many legs it has—which moves first when it begins to run?
Confused by it all, it is completely immobilized. It can't run—in
fact, it can't move because it can't decide which leg to activate
first.

It's a suggestive picture, and it hints at what James is telling us.
We are not immobilized. We move all right—but we cannot
decide our movement if we are double-minded. To change the
metaphor, we are like a wave on the sea, driven not by our will,
but by the will of the wind. What a picture of the bottom line of
such a life: A double-minded person, unstable in all ways, will
not receive anything from the Lord.

A university freshman was about to go on her first blind date.
Her roommate was making all the arrangements and asked
whether she preferred southern boys or northern boys.

A Midwesterner, the freshman was innocently unaware of such
subtle distinctions and asked, "What is the difference?"

Her worldly wise roommate answered, "Southern boys are
more romantic. They will take you walking in the moonlight and
whisper sweet nothings in your ear. Northern boys are more
active. They like to go places and do exciting things."

The girl pondered the contrast and then asked wistfully,
"Could you please find me a southern boy from as far north as
possible?"

We want to negotiate in the same fashion. We are double-
minded, like Bunyan's character, Mr. Facing Both Ways. Even if
we aren't immobilized, we certainly aren't clear about direction.

> *"The double-minded person becomes a walking civil war."*

Well, how do we escape? How do we break out of this half-and-half life, this double-mindedness?

First, we must learn to say no.

Now, don't think that's so simple you do not pay it any attention. Let me underscore it. We *must* learn to say no. In his column, Russell Baker claims that in the English language, "no" is the hardest word to say. According to Baker, one of the worst mistakes he ever made was throwing away a brochure from an agent who was trying to establish himself in a unique business—he would say "no" for you. That's all he did to earn his fee—he said no. Baker went on:

> Some people are strong enough to say no for themselves, but they are a minority. If everyone who wanted to say no had the strength to do it, human activity in the United States would probably drop by 90%. The number of weddings would decrease, crime would decline, and Sunday dinner with the whole darn family would be a dying institution.

If we are not going to be wishy-washy, we must learn to say no.

But there's more. We must learn to say *yes.* The Greek word James uses is *dipsuchos,* translated "double-minded." The word literally means a person with two souls or two minds. One mind believes; the other disbelieves. The double-minded person becomes a walking civil war, in whch trust and distrust of God wage a continual battle.

We must learn to say *Yes—Yes,* with all our being—to God. We can't mess with Mr. In-between.

There are so many issues in life that would be settled, that would not drain us of the energy involved in decision-making, if we would settle once and for all who we are and whose we are.

Going back to the story of Dr. Hendrick Kramer, what power is in that symbol—*picking up the Bible!* And how clearly the bottom line is etched in Kramer's word: "I cannot tell you what to do, but I can tell you who you are."

The alternative to saying yes to God is always destructive. When James says that the double-minded person is unstable, I get a picture of a drunken person, staggering from side to side on the road, but getting nowhere. Saying yes to God gives us that steady movement we need, that strength to withstand the storms, that sense of what is right and the will to do it.

Then we can say *no* to what is not in keeping with God's will, not in harmony with our Christian commitment. We can say *no* to that which hurts another person. We can say *no* to the passions of our flesh which give us pleasure for a season, but threaten the values that sustain life and provide stability. We can say *no* to the attractive shortcuts that deceive us, *no* to the invitation to cut a corner here and a corner there, knowing that there are no shortcuts to decency and honor and obedience and holiness.

Have you noticed this phenomenon? When we say a solid *yes* to God, we are given discernment as to what we should say *no* to, and the power to say it. And then our *no* to those things becomes a *yes* to God.

Following a concert by famous violinist Fritz Kreisler, a woman from the audience came backstage to greet him. "I'd give my life to play as beautifully as you do," she said.

He replied, "I did."

That's the picture. No messing with Mr. In-between. For the double-minded person, "unstable in every way, must not expect to receive anything from the Lord." We must say *yes* to God, and keep on saying it, until we are able to say *no* to all that God says no to.

Here is a suggestion for putting this lesson of James into practice: Before you say yes to anything, ask yourself, Is this a *yes* to God? And when you are confronted with a questionable act, a confusing situation, ask yourself, Is this something God would say *no* to? Let your yes's and no's be expressions of who you are.

CHAPTER THREE

> *Let the lowly brother boast in his exaltation, and the rich in his humiliation, because like the flower of the grass he will pass away. For the sun rises with its scorching heat and withers the grass; its flower falls, and its beauty perishes. So will the rich man fade away in the midst of his pursuits.*
> *(James 1:9-11 RSV)*

How to Be Rich and Poor

O ne day Herman and Clara were riding along in their shiny new car. Clara spoke up and said, "You know, Herman, if it weren't for my money, we probably wouldn't have this wonderful new car." Herman just sat there and didn't say a word.

They pulled into their driveway, and Herman turned off the engine. As they quietly admired their beautiful home, Clara said, "You know, Herman, if it weren't for my money, we probably wouldn't have this house." Herman just sat there and didn't say a word.

That afternoon, a delivery truck pulled up in front of the house, and the men brought in a brand new piano. It was placed in the living room where its shiny finish caught the rays of the afternoon sun.

"You know, Herman," said Clara once more, "if it weren't for my money, we probably wouldn't have this piano." Once more, Herman just sat there and didn't say a word.

Later that night, Herman and Clara prepared to go to bed. As they pulled up the covers of the bed, Clara paused, and then in a reflective mood, said, "You know, Herman, if it weren't for my money, why we wouldn't have the dresser in this room, or the corner table, and we wouldn't have this warm, comfortable bed."

With that, poor old Herman turned to Clara and said, "I don't want to hurt your feelings, Honey, but you know, just like the car, the house, the piano, the dresser, the table, and this bed—if it weren't for your money, I wouldn't be here either!"

Where would we be if it weren't for money? Whether we are talking about our own money or someone else's, that's an important question. But more important is the question, Where are we *with* our money? The asking of such questions, or even thinking in that way, suggests that I'm talking about a lot of money. But not so. I'm talking about money, period—a little or a lot. I'm talking about how to be rich and poor.

That's the way James talked about it. Is anything more practical than money? Can we consider practical Christianity without considering money? Is there a more pressing question for the Christian than how to relate to money and how to use what we have? Our attitude toward money is a major factor in determining how we live our lives.

Nothing confirms the assumption that the Epistle of James is a how-to book than the way James talks about money. He addresses the question from a broad perspective—not one-sidedly, not from a narrow point of view. He is telling us how to be rich and how to be poor. So he is not out to gouge the conscience of the rich or pour more sympathy on the poor. He is dealing with Christians—all Christians. Some may be rich; certainly many are poor. Whatever the economic state, attitude is the key: God gave—So You Can.

> *"What we have does not determine whether we have the Kingdom."*

A friend, Norman Neaves, tells of a recent experience. A husband and wife, new members of the congregation, came up to him at a social gathering at the church.

They said they had just sold one of their businesses, and they didn't want to profit from it without sharing a good portion with the Lord. So they handed Norm a check—the second such check they had given since they had been members of the church. He was astounded to see that, once again, it was in the amount of $10,000!

With tears in his eyes, the husband said, "Twenty-five years ago, I was almost dead. I had 19 operations in 12 years, and the Lord pulled me through." And then he added, "I am just grateful to be alive and to be here today!"

Not that dramatically—but if we all stopped and thought about how much God gives us—then there would be no question about whether we can give.

The word of James that we are considering is a tough one. James shares practical advice for those who are rich as well as for those who are poor. He recognizes that riches may be a problem for the rich who believe that money is everything, and it may be a problem for the poor who have come to believe that their needs can be met if they only had more money. So he is talking to the rich *and* the poor. Thus our theme: *How to be rich and poor.*

Let's seek to learn from James by first considering a bold assertion: *What we have does not determine whether we have the Kingdom.* James begins by addressing the poor: "Let the lowly brother boast in his exaltation" (1:9). The message is clear. Those who find themselves in humble circumstances or a low position can take pride in the fact that a high position awaits them in the Kingdom of God. We used to sing an old gospel hymn down in Perry County, Mississippi:

This world is not my home,
I'm just a-passing through,
My treasures are laid up,
somewhere beyond the blue.
The angels beckon me from heaven's open door,
And I can't feel at home in this world anymore.

The word the Revised Standard Version translates "boast" is rendered "glory" in the King James Version, and "brag" by Barclay. That raises some questions. Are we to boast, or brag, or glory in the fact that we are poor? Not at all. There is an emotional and spiritual sickness that takes pride in poverty. And there is an even worse sickness in the soul of those who would twist scripture to fit their own station in life—especially to condescendingly think that poor people should be happy with what they have.

That's not what James is saying. He is calling lowly Christians—the poor—to rejoice in the fact that their lowly estate is temporary. *What we have does not determine whether we have the Kingdom.*

The marvelous spirituals that were sung and cherished by slaves had this perspective. Those songs were songs of rejoicing—not in slavery, but in the fact that their status in life was temporary. You remember "Swing Low, Sweet Chariot." Here's the last verse of that spiritual:

I'm sometimes up, I'm sometimes down,
Comin' for to carry me home.
But still my soul is heavenward-bound,
Comin' for to carry me home.

Sometimes the conditions were so tough, they prayed for the change to come soon—"I want to cross over into Campground." Well, it was not just the slaves who received this message that we can glory in the fact that our lowly estate is short-lived. We poor whites in rural Mississippi sang our hope too. Almost as soon as I could talk, I was singing with the rest. Not only "This World Is Not My Home"—but another just like it:

When we all get to heaven,
What a day of rejoicing that will be.
When we all see Jesus,
We'll sing and shout the Victory!

God has invited all of us to the riches of the Kingdom. We may be passing through difficult times, we may think there's no escape, but there's going to be a "great getting-up morning"— again to use the words of the spiritual—and loyal subjects of the King of Kings and Lord of Lords will be welcomed into the Kingdom of God. We will have positions as exalted as any others.

James is telling us that even though we may be poor, we can be rich—rich in the things that really matter—rich in the Kingdom sense. And that doesn't mean only the inheritance of an eternal Kingdom, though that's the focus of James.

There are Kingdom values that can be ours now, regardless of our possessions. What we have does not determine whether we have the Kingdom.

> *"The value of what we have is determined by whether we have the Kingdom."*

Some time ago, a poignant story appeared in the *Los Angeles Times*. It told of a young woman who had learned that truth in her head but failed to believe it enough to carry her through her despair. She got into her Mercedes 450-SL and drove away to die. The life she chose to leave was a life many people would have envied. She was attractive, successful, wealthy, but she chose to end a life in which, she wrote, she was "so tired of clapping with one hand."

In a special note to close friends, she said: "Just do me a favor so this won't all be for nothing. Don't let the pursuit of money and success interfere in the beautiful relationship you two have. As long as you have each other and a strong faith in God, you'll want for nothing else."

So Jesus' words abide: "Don't store up for *yourselves treasures on earth where moth and rust* corrupt and thieves break in and steal; instead, store up for yourselves treasures in heaven. . . . As I *have loved you, so you also ought to love one* another."

So James is teaching us how to be rich and poor. He first addresses a word to the poor. That was the first truth: What we have doesn't determine whether we have the Kingdom. Now a second truth: *The value of what we have is determined by whether we have the Kingdom.*

Now he speaks to the rich: "Let the lowly brother boast in his exaltation, and the rich in his humiliation, because like the flower of the grass he will pass away" (1:9-10).

That is a tough word. On the surface, it may seem contradictory—the rich are to glory, or to boast, in their humiliation.

That's a contradiction, isn't it—to boast in humiliation? That's impossible. Yes, on the human level. It goes against everything the world teaches us about the power and the glory of riches. But James is using "Kingdom" talk. His perspective is that of the Kingdom of God.

In the Kingdom, when the Kingdom really gets hold of us, we receive a new sense of perspective in relation to life and to God. We come to know that life is a gift, that we don't *earn* that which enriches our lives. It is all Grace.

> *"The great peril of riches is that they tend to bring us a false sense of security."*

It's interesting to note that the Greek word translated "humiliation," in verse 10, is the same root word used in verse 9 to describe the brother who is lowly. What a tremendous insight! God has asked the brother who is *lowly* to *glory* in his exalted state in the Kingdom, while he asks the rich man to *glory* in his *humble estate* in relation to God.

He is putting us all in the same place in relation to God: poor, in that our need is for God; rich, in that we are offered all the abundance of God's grace. You see, the value of what we have—even of who we are—is determined by whether we have the Kingdom.

That brings us back to the big question, which is our theme for this study: How to be rich and poor.

The one big lesson in this word of James is *we must realize and acknowledge our utter dependency upon God.* Now, many of us resist that. We are like Charlie Brown's little sister, Sally.

She said to Charlie in one of the cartoons, "I'm doomed! I need to write a report on rivers, and it's due next week, and I know I'm going to fail!"

Charlie Brown responded, "Well, why don't you work real hard and turn in the best report you can possibly write?"

To that, Sally meekly replied, "You know, that never occurred to me!"

Has it ever occurred to you that we are utterly dependent upon God? James makes that case especially strong as it relates to the rich. He knows that the great peril of riches is that they tend to bring us a false sense of security. Having wealth causes people to feel safe, to feel that they have resources to cope with anything—that they can buy anything they want, even buy themselves out of any situation they might wish to escape.

James draws a vivid picture, which would have been very familiar to the people in Palestine. In the desert, if there is a shower of rain, the thin green shoots of grass will sprout. Yet one day's burning sunshine will make them vanish as if they had never been.

James is saying that as the grass and flower wilt, and their beauty comes to an end with the scorching sun, so "will the rich man fade away in the midst of his pursuits."

This is the same message that Jesus sounded. In his parable of the sower, he describes the seed that fell among the thorns, "But the cares of the world, and the delight in riches, and the desire for other things, enter in and choke the word, and it proves unfruitful" (Mark 4:19 RSV).

I heard recently of a woman who went into a coffee shop and sat down, not disturbing the gentleman sitting at the same table. She opened her purse and took out a magazine and started to read. After a bit, she reached for one of the cookies that were in a bag sitting on the table. And when she did, the man reached and took a cookie too. This made the woman angry, and she glared at him, though he turned and smiled very kindly at her.

Moments later, the same thing happened again. She reached for a cookie and he reached for a cookie at the same time. It made her furious that he should be doing that, and she glared again, though he simply smiled.

Finally the woman got up to leave and walked angrily past the man and out to the elevators in the lobby. Then it happened! As she was standing there, still fuming, she opened her purse to put her magazine back inside. And do you know what she discovered? She discovered that her bag of cookies, unopened, was still in her purse!

You see, she had been eating the man's cookies all along—and she thought that he had been eating hers!

> *"When we withhold the tithe,*
> *we are robbing God."*

Isn't that the way it is with us? We eat God's "cookies" without acknowledging, without being aware that we are utterly dependent upon God. We think that what we have is ours, and we can do with it as we please. Tithing our income is an issue here. When the prophet Malachi asked, "Will anyone rob God?" (3:8 NRSV), he was making the point that everything belongs to God. When we withhold the tithe, we are robbing God.

Though not explicitly, James is teaching us a lesson in contentment. Rather than pursuing things we do not have, as those who have little are apt to do, and rather than trusting in things, as those who are rich are apt to do, we are invited, as Hebrews 13, verse 5, puts it, to "Keep your life free from love of money, and be content with what you have; for he has said, 'I will never leave you nor forsake you'" (RSV).

The apostle Paul teaches us that the person who is truly rich is the person who has learned to be content. Do you remember his word to the Philippians?

"Not that I complain of want; for I have learned, in whatever state I am, to be content. I know how to be abased, and I know how to abound; in any and all circumstances I have learned the secret of facing plenty and hunger, abundance and want" (4:11-12 RSV).

He concluded by saying, "I can do all things through him who strengthens me" (4:13 RSV).

Whatever our earthly estate, the best is yet to come. The Lord is to be trusted. His Kingdom will come, and if we trust and follow him, we will be a part of that Kingdom.

So, James teaches us how to be rich and poor. He gives us four valuable lessons for a practical Christian approach to our attitude and our use of material possessions:

One—What we have does not determine whether we have the Kingdom.

Two—The value of what we have is determined by whether we have the Kingdom.

Three—We must realize and acknowledge our dependence on God.

Four—The person who is rich, in the richest sense, is the one who has learned to be content in any circumstance.

CHAPTER FOUR

Blessed is anyone who endures temptation. Such a one has stood the test and will receive the crown of life that the Lord has promised to those who love him. No one, when tempted, should say, "I am being tempted by God"; for God cannot be tempted by evil and he himself tempts no one. But one is tempted by one's own desire, being lured and enticed by it; then, when that desire has conceived, it gives birth to sin, and that sin, when it is fully grown, gives birth to death.
(James 1:12-15 NRSV)

Meeting and Mastering Temptation

A man went to his counselor about a personal problem: "I have a real struggle here. I feel as if I'm violating my conscience. I'm not being completely honest with myself."

The counselor said to him, "Well, would you like to see me about strengthening your will power?"

The man thought for a moment, then replied, "No, what I would like to talk to you about is weakening my conscience."

That reflects our age, doesn't it? We are not so much interested in developing our conscience as in finding a way to live the way we wish without feeling guilty.

In Paris, another man, extremely depressed, went to see a psychiatrist. The man's eyes were sunken and his cheeks were hollow. His back was stooped and his body was emaciated. His hands trembled and his face was unshaven. He told the doctor that he had lost his zip in life, that he didn't feel as if he wanted to live anymore.

The doctor said to him, "I have the solution for you. You need to go and look up Grimaldi, the playboy. He knows how to have a good time. He knows how to get the most out of life. He will show you how to start living again, how to really enjoy yourself."

There was a long pause, and then, with incredibly depressed eyes, the man looked up at the psychiatrist.

"Doctor," he said very quietly, "I am Grimaldi."

Those two stories tell *the* story—the story of our predicament. We'd like to live as we please, but we can't. That is, we can't if we wish to have meaning and deep joy—if we want to please God and inherit the eternal life God promises.

> *"God does not allow temptation in order to threaten our faith, but to deepen it."*

James speaks to the issue. At the core of what he says is a great message about meeting and mastering temptation. The key principle is this: God does not allow temptation in order to threaten our faith, but to deepen it. So how to meet and master temptation is of paramount importance to Christians.

But first the question, Why does God allow temptation? An answer is found in the meaning of the Greek word for temptation, *pierasmos.* Selwyn Hughes gives an excellent explanation, in *How to Live the Christian Life:*

It means to test, to try, or to prove. The biblical use of the word, unlike the modern use of it, does not contain the thought of seduction or entrapment, but rather the putting of a person to a test for the purpose of deepening personal qualities. This then is the purpose behind temptation—it is God's way of helping us to deepen inward qualities and develop our character. Dr. Oswald Chambers says, "God can, in one single moment, make a heart pure, but not even God himself can give a person *character*." It is essential that we are subjected to testing, for character would not be the precious thing it is if it could be acquired without effort, without combat and without contradictions. "Virtue that has not been tried," said one great theologian, "does not deserve the name of virtue."

The word for *temptation* literally means "to put to the test" or "to go through." To tempt means to entice, essay, examine, or try. Temptation, then, is a putting to proof—for good, or an evil solicitation—for bad.

We need to recognize, then, that temptation can be used for our good or for our harm. This certainly harmonizes with James' word in verse 12: "Blessed is anyone who endures temptation. Such a one has stood the test and will receive the crown of life that the Lord has promised to those who love him." One of God's uses of temptation is to bring us to maturity in Christ.

> *"Even in temptation, God is working in us to bring us to full maturity in Christ."*

Gerald Manley Hopkins was an English poet who was converted to the Roman Catholic Church, became a Jesuit priest, and was sent to Dublin to teach in the University College. He was a great poet—not easy to read, but the kind of poet who influenced other poets. The next generation of English poets, among them T. S. Eliot and W. H. Auden, acknowledged their indebtedness to Hopkins. He wrote a marvelous poem titled "Long Live the Weeds," in which he confirmed what we are talking about here:

Long live the weeds that overwhelm
my narrow vegetable realm;
The bitter rock, the barren soil
that force the Son of Man to toil;
All things unholy marred by a curse,
the ugly of the universe.
The rough, the wicked, and the wild,
that keeps the spirit undefiled.
With these I match my little wit
and earn the right to stand and sit.
Hope, love, create, or drink and die:
These shape the creature that is I.

It's beautiful exposition of the biblical understanding of life. We don't understand the presence of weeds in our lives, nor the bitter rock, nor the barren soil. Weeds and rocks are just there. And, interestingly, the Bible offers no real explanation for these things. But the witness of the scripture is clear. None of these things—none of these sufferings, none of this absurdity—is able to defeat us, to overcome God's will in our life. In fact, the Bible says that God is able to use the weeds themselves for our good and his glory.

So even in temptation, God is working in us to bring us to full maturity in Christ. Temptation, testing, and trials—and the way we endure them—may be used by God.

Think back to the temptation of Christ. Certainly that experience in the wilderness strengthened him and brought him forth in the power of the Spirit. The experience produced a single-minded allegiance to God. Moffatt's translation of the moment when Jesus rebuted Satan's temptation in the wilderness, as recorded in Matthew 4:10-11, reads: " 'Begone, Satan! it is written, You must worship the Lord your God, and serve him *alone.*' At this the devil left him" (italics mine).

The way Moffatt translates this passage seems to suggest that when Jesus used the word *alone,* the devil left him. One commentator says of this translation that Satan could not stand that word *alone,* and when Jesus uttered it, he turned and left because he knew that to tempt a man who stands on that word, in single-minded allegiance to God, is only to strengthen that man and deepen, rather than destroy, his confidence in the Almighty.

So, temptation may be used by God to bring us to maturity in Christ.

> *"Our trials and temptations*
> *propel us to prayer."*

Trials, testing, and temptation also play a major role in developing our prayer life. Martin Luther claimed that his temptations were his "Masters of Divinity," which taught him more about prayer than all his formal training as a priest.

Many of us can identify with the notion of prayer as a battleground. It's here that we bring the fighting forces and passions of our life into God's presence. It's here that we seek the Spirit's power—not to referee the raging conflicts, but to resolve them.

Most of us pray at times when we feel we need it most. Our trials and temptations propel us to prayer, turn us in the direction of God's throne of grace. The pressure and luring invitations from the evil one call for power not our own, so we pray.

Move now to another point of truth, which I state in this fashion: God allows temptation, but he does not allow us to be tempted beyond the point of no return.

This is the way Paul put it in I Corinthians: "No temptation has overtaken you that is not common to man. God is faithful, and he will not let you be tempted beyond your strength, but with the temptation will also provide the way of escape, that you may be able to endure it" (10:13 RSV).

Isn't that a great word? So we need to keep that perspective. God does not allow us to be tempted beyond the point of no return.

In Andrew Greeley's novel *Patience of a Saint,* there is a character named Red Cain, a rough, hard-living reporter in Chicago. Then Cain undergoes a dramatic conversion experience, which he describes as being zapped by God. But after his shattering spiritual breakthrough, instead of things getting better for him, they go from bad to worse. His family turns away from him. He loses his job. A novel he has written is rejected.

Frustrated and disgusted with what he considers being let down by God, he goes to his pastor and seeks assurance that God will reward him for changing the direction of his life.

But his pastor tells him, "The Lord offers no guarantees." His novel may be rejected again, he may not find another job, and reconciliation with his family may take a long time.

Afraid that he might lose everything, Red Cain says to himself, "If God expects that kind of courage from anyone, then God should provide some guarantees."

Well, God does provide guarantees—but not the kind of guarantee most of us wish for. The guarantee is not that the testing will not come. God's guarantee is this: Every temptation that we face is common to others, and God is faithful. He can be trusted.

God will not allow us to be tempted beyond what we are able to stand. God's strength is greater than any alluring temptation.

Have you considered the fullness of James's claim? With the temptation, God will make a way of escape. To trust Christ is not to have a life free of trials and temptations, but to have the confidence that "greater is He that is within you than he that is in the world." So rehearse what we have considered:

One—temptation has a purpose.

Two—God does not tempt us, but allows temptation, and for a very particular purpose: to develop our character; to bring us to a single-minded allegiance to God; and to develop our prayer life.

Three—Though God allows us to be tempted, he does not allow it beyond the point of no return.

CHAPTER FIVE

> *Do not be deceived, my beloved. Every generous act of giving, with every perfect gift, is from above, coming down from the Father of lights, with whom there is no variation or shadow due to change. In fulfillment of his own purpose he gave us birth by the word of truth, so that we would become a kind of first fruits of his creatures. (James 1:16-18 NRSV)*

Will the Real God Please Stand?

A young theological student was having a difficult time describing his relationship with God, so the counselor asked the young man to draw a picture that would illustrate the way he thought of God. The student said he couldn't draw very well, so he would do it at home and bring it back when the class met again the next week.

It happened to be around Christmastime, and when the seminary student returned, he brought an artist's drawing of an extra-large, angry, demanding Scrooge-type person, sitting behind a desk with pen in hand and his debit-credit ledger before him. In front of Scrooge, standing in terror, was Bob Cratchett.

Pointing to Scrooge, the young man said, "That's God." Pointing to Cratchett, he said, "That's me."

40

We cringe at the thought of such a God, but do we feel with the young man? In all of us, there is probably some difference in the way we talk about God, in our mental/philosophical concepts of God, and how we feel deep down about God. As another way to say it, the God of our minds may not be the same as the God of our feelings.

How we feel about God is the most determinative factor in our relationship with God. It's not surprising that many Christians know who God is and what God is like; and yet, deep down, in the levels of their emotions, there exists a very different feeling and picture of God. That deep-down feeling prevents really lasting spiritual growth and victory in our lives.

Joseph Seka has written a helpful article, "Will the Real God Please Stand Up?" That's where I got the title for this chapter. In that article, Mr. Seka lists some of the faulty concepts and feelings about God found among both Christians and non-Christians:

> First, there is the legal god. This god keeps account of what we do and waits for us to step out of line. . . .
> Second, the "Gotcha god" resembles Sherlock Holmes. . . . Like a private investigator, he's always following and gathering evidence.
> Third, there is the Sitting Bull god. This god sits in the yoga position and expects burnt offerings . . . .
> Fourth, there is the philosopher god. . . . He is distant, cold, too-busy, and has a "Do not disturb" sign on his office.
> Last, there is the pharaoh god. . . . He is harsh and demanding, and says, "Make more bricks."

Now, not many of us would describe God in any of these ways, but isn't it true that at the feeling level, we perceive God in at least some of these ways—a God who keeps account of what we do; a God who expects us to try to please him all the time; a God who has a "Do Not Disturb" sign on his office door; a God who is always demanding more than we can give.

The truth is this: Developing a healthy, truthful experience of God, harmonized in thought and feeling, is an ongoing growth process that comes with maturity in Christ.

> *"God never lets us down; God never lets us off; God never lets us go."*

So let's think and feel about God under the rubric of our text from James. We are familiar with the first part of verse 17: "Every generous act of giving, with every perfect gift, is from above." But what about the second part: "coming down from the Father of lights, with whom there is no variation or shadow due to change" (NRSV).

The King James Version has: "cometh down from the Father of lights, with whom is no variableness, neither shadow of turning."

That's a wonderful phrase—"neither shadow of turning." It's descriptive of the real God, who will stand from the pages of the Bible when you take the book as a whole, and especially when you look through the lens of the Incarnation. In him there is no variableness, neither shadow of turning.

These words of James say three things about the nature of God. First, God is the Father of lights, the Creator of this universe. Second, with God there is no variation, or change. And third, with God, there is no shadow of turning. This teaches us that God is everlastingly faithful. Turning is what casts shadows. It is because the Earth is turning that the sun goes down and shadows appear.

Now I want to put these three truths about the nature of God together, and out of them, sound three affirmations, as suggested by Alan Redhead: One, God never lets us down; two, God never lets us off; and three, God never lets us go.

First, God never lets us down. God is the Father, James says, and the love of our Father-God never lets us down. Listen to Jesus as the authorized spokesman of God, and look at what Jesus did as the life of God, and you can't deny the fact that God never lets us down. Instead of letting folks down, Jesus was always lifting them up.

There are times, of course, when it seems that God lets us

42

down. We pray for a passing grade on an examination and don't get it. We pray for a job but someone else gets it. We ask to be delivered from some crippling handicap, but remain limited by it; no deliverance comes. A loved one is smitten by divorce. We pray for healing, but are grief-stricken by death.

As Alan Redhead put it, "We seek a detour around the road with a cross at the end of it, but find all of the roads are closed." Sometimes it does seem as if God lets us down. It even seemed so to his own Son, once. "My God, my God," he cried, "Why hast thou forsaken me?"

> *"Whenever we mash a finger or have a flat tire, the cry goes up that God has let us down."*

And all the while, the reason for our thinking so is our self-centeredness. We put ourselves at the center of the universe and expect God to regard us as such, to make it his chief business to look after us. We count him our private property—our personal nursemaid, if you will, who has nothing to do but watch our interests and save us from trouble. And so, whenever we mash our finger or have a flat tire, the cry goes up that God has let us down. In *Getting to Know God,* Alan Redhead suggests:

> That is to misunderstand God. God never promised to save anybody from trouble, not even his own Son. We are not the center of the universe. God is the center. His eternal purpose, not our personal pleasure, is the big thing.
>
> But though God never promised to save anybody from trouble, he does promise to save us *in* trouble. That is a promise you can count on, and it will not let you down. He "preparest a table before me in the presence of mine enemies." That reminds us to a word which war put into our vocabulary—"logistics." It means the service by which fighting forces are kept supplied with what they need to do battle. God has a service of supply too, and with respect to logistics you can know that God never lets you down. (p. 32)

God never lets us down.

But that isn't all. If we stop there, we will not be inviting the real God to stand up. Though God never lets us down, he never lets us off. Judgment is a fact of life.

Playwright T. S. Eliot expressed the stark realism of that: "Of all that was done in the past, you eat the fruit, either rotten or ripe. . . . For every ill deed in the past, we suffer the consequences."

Some would say that the love of God is not soft like a jellyfish. It has backbone. That's true. But the image can be expanded. Though seemingly flabby and harmless, the jellyfish has a burning sting.

God is love, yet God is holy. God's moral demands are as certain in their call upon our life, never letting us off, as his love is certain in never letting us down.

James called God the Father of lights. Light suggests openness and judgment. Under God's light, all that is is illuminated. We can't be sentimental about it. God is not a "yes person," who winks at sin and says it doesn't matter. When you look at God through the person of Christ, you know that, along with the tenderness of God, comes also the terror of God.

As Redhead says, "It is not that God finds any pleasure in punishing sin. It is just that there is something in God called holiness, and that holiness sets up a law which says that right is right and wrong is wrong, and wrong must be punished. Not even God can repeal that law."

It was Jesus, God's Love Incarnate, who said, "Be not deceived; God is not mocked: for whatsoever a man soweth, that shall he also reap."

And now the final word: God never lets us go.

Here is the greatest word that can be spoken about love. It keeps on loving, in spite of everything. It takes no account of the wrongs done against it. No matter how often its offers are spurned, no matter how often its favors are refused, no matter how poignantly it is wounded or how far away the loved one wanders. It always holds on, never gives up, never lets go.

Where do we get this picture? In Jesus Christ. The one thing we see about God in Christ is that he never gives up, never lets us go.

Chapter 15 of Luke has been called the Gospel Within the Gospel, for there Jesus tells three stories which reveal the nature of God: God is like the woman who searched every corner for the lost coin; God is like the shepherd who would not abandon one lost sheep; God is like the father who rejoiced in the return of his ungrateful son.

God never lets us go.

John Powell is a professor of theology at Loyola University in Chicago. One of my most meaningful experiences was doing a film interview with Father John—and out of that interview he published a little book titled *He Touched Me.*

John is a powerful communicator. I heard him tell a story about a former student who begrudgingly took one of his theology courses. The boy's name was Tommy, and he didn't want to study theology, but it was a required course.

At the end of the last class, Tommy asked, "Professor Powell, do you think I will ever find God?" Well, Powell knew all too well that Tommy not only was cynical about God, but that he also was the self-appointed "atheist in residence."

Powell thought for a moment, then replied, "No, I don't. I don't think you will ever find God, Tommy—but I am absolutely certain that God will find you!"

And with that, Tommy left the classroom and the two did not see each other for some time. Then one day, quite by surprise, Tommy walked into John Powell's office. He looked different. He *was* different. He told Powell that he had a terminal illness and did not have long to live. His once youthful body had already started to deteriorate, but his eyes were bright, and his face was aglow. This is what he said to Father Powell:

> What I really came to see you about was what you said to me on the last day of class. When the doctors removed the lump and told me it was malignant, well, I got real serious about locating God. . . . I really began banging bloody fists against the doors of heaven. But God did not come out. In fact, nothing happened.

45

But then something did happen. Tommy had not really had a close relationship with this father, and the thought occurred to him that he might die before he ever expressed his love to his father. So he went home, and now told Powell the story: "My dad was reading the newspaper. It was very difficult, but I finally said the words. 'Dad, I love you—that's all. I just wanted you to know that.' The newspaper fluttered to the floor. Then my father did two things I could never remember him ever doing before. He cried, and he hugged me. And we talked all night."

Then Tommy said these final words to John Powell: "One day I turned around, and Father Powell, God was there. He didn't come to me when I pleaded with him. But the important thing is that he found me."

And it will be so—for any one of us, and, I hope, for all of us. For God never lets us go.

Could it be expressed any more clearly? God never lets us down, never lets us off, and never lets us go!

CHAPTER SIX

> *Let everyone be quick to listen, slow to speak, slow to anger; for your anger does not produce God's righteousness. (James 1:19b-20 NRSV)*
>
> *The tongue is a small member, yet it boasts of great exploits. How great a forest is set ablaze by a small fire! And the tongue is a fire. (James 3:5-6a NRSV)*

Swift to Hear— Slow to Speak

Four women, playing bridge in the recreation room of a retirement center in California, were chatting more than paying attention to their game, when they noticed an older gentleman wander into the room. None of them had seen him before. He was obviously a newcomer.

Quickly, the four ladies perked up. One said, "Well, hello there. You're new here, aren't you?"

The old man smiled and responded, "Just moved in this morning."

A second lady spoke. "Well, where did you come from? Where did you live before?"

Matter-of-factly came the reply: "San Quentin. I was just released from there. I've been there for thirty years."

"Oh, is that right?" said the third lady. "What were you in for?" Without even hesitating a moment, the old man answered, "I murdered my wife."

The fourth lady sat up in her chair. Her eyes sparkled, and she gave him a big smile as she said, "Oh, then that means you're single."

It's true, isn't it? More often than not, we hear what we want to hear. Communication is crucial. And certainly, when we talk about practical Christianity, as we are doing here, we need to talk about communication.

James talks about it. He addresses the problem and gives us a one-line lesson. You have heard of the "one-minute manager." Here is a 5-second lesson in communication—that is, the lesson is stated in 5 seconds. We learn it and live it over a lifetime. Nothing we've learned about communication exceeds the wisdom of James: "Let everyone be quick to listen, slow to speak."

Did you note that James mentions hearing before he talks about speaking? Does that mean that listening is more important than speaking? I don't know, but I do know that most of us talk more than we listen.

Bruce Larsen once quipped, "It makes me angry to hear the words, 'Next time we get together, I want to hear all about you!'"

I can understand that. I share Bruce's anger. I have two clergy friends whom I see only once or twice a year. It happened recently that I saw them both in the course of a couple of weeks. They live on either side of the continent, and we meet only when we gather for other events. It dawned on me, after those two visits, that neither of those friends had asked about my family. I had talked about their children—all of them adults. And they had responded, glowingly. I learned all that was going on— some of it was good; some of it was bad. But later I became · angry. Some big and deep things were going on in the Dunnam family, and they didn't even ask!

So I can understand Bruce's anger. To care about others is to listen to them. There are few greater insults than to talk to a person and discover that that person is not only not listening to you, but is not even looking at you.

Think about it. Most of us talk more than we listen.

The second thing I know is that all of us need someone who listens and hears us.

Despite all the talk and emphasis placed on communication today, Donald Shelby reminds us that listening and hearing do not happen between persons. Our technology has provided us with a means to listen in the depths of oceans, listen to distant planets, and listen to the first signals from extraterrestrial beings (we can even look at and listen to the baby in the womb). We can listen to plants and to our brain waves, but we seldom listen to each other. We need people who actively listen to us until they hear us; who are with us, not just alongside us; who realize that often what we say is not what we mean; who listen until they hear the deeper, unspoken meanings and yearnings we do not or cannot express. All of us need someone who listens and hears us.

> *"Most of us would be amazed by how much more effective we would be in our witnessing if we stopped talking and began to listen."*

In studying the earthly life of Jesus as reported in the Gospels, we are deeply touched by his marvelous ability to listen. While his disciples were arguing and talking, Jesus was listening to their deeper needs and those of the people they encountered.

He traveled the same roads and village streets as his contemporaries, yet he heard and saw needs that no one else seemed to notice. Why was this so? Authentic love. His love and compassion motivated him to listen. How could he express caring without knowing the thoughts and feelings of others? He heard not only words but nonverbal communication. So he was constantly meeting people at their point of need.

Think about a woman at the well in Samaria, the blind beggar, Bartimaeus in Jericho, or Zacchaeus up a sycamore tree. They were the recipients of his ministry because he listened to them closely enough to really hear.

He invites us to the ministry of listening. Most of us would be amazed by how much more effective we would be in our witnessing if we stopped talking and began to listen.

Everybody has a story. How are we to convincingly invite others to consider the story of Jesus unless we can let them know that his story fits into theirs. The most effective means of ministry is listening and responding to need, not dumping our load.

The chances are that we will not have the commitment and discipline to listen to others until and unless we cultivate listening to Jesus.

Using the analogy of our being the sheep and his being our Shepherd, he said, "When he has brought out all his own, he goes ahead of them, and the sheep follow him because they know his voice. They will not follow a stranger, but they will run from him because they do not know the voice of strangers" (John 10:4-5 NRSV).

In the same way a sheep listens to its shepherd's voice, we should become increasingly acquainted with the voice of our Lord. As we listen more closely to him, his compassion and care "rubs off" on us, and we begin to listen to others more intentionally.

But what about talking? James says that we are to be slow to talk. James T. Clellan, a Presbyterian minister, says that we are living in an age of "gobbledegook," "bafflegab," "officialeese, with its abandonment of simplicity, its pseudo-learned vocabulary, its capacity to abuse, to mutilate, even to murder the King's English."

Then he tells the hilarious story of a plumber who wrote to the national Bureau of Standards. The plumber said he had found that hydrochloric acid opens plugged pipes quickly and asked whether it was a good thing for a plumber to use.

A scientist at the bureau replied as follows: "The uncertain reactive processes of hydrochloric acid places pipes in jeopardy when alkalinity is involved. The efficiency of this solution is disputable, but the corrosive residue is incompatible with metallic permanence."

The plumber wrote back, thanking the bureau for telling him

that this method was all right. The scientist was disturbed about the misunderstanding and showed the correspondence to his boss—another scientist—who immediately wrote the plumber: "Hydrochloric acid generates a toxic and noxious residue which will produce submuriate invalidating reactions. Consequently, some alternative procedure is preferable."

The plumber wrote back that he agreed with the bureau— "Hydrochloric acid works just fine." Greatly disturbed, the two scientists took their problem to the top boss. The next day the plumber received this telegram: "Don't use hydrochloric acid. It eats hell out of the pipes!"

When we are slow to talk, we don't contribute to the gobbledegook, bafflegab, and officialeese that is drowning us in words.

That brings us to the second part of our scripture lesson— James 3:5-6 (NRSV).

In verse 26 of the first chapter, James had said, "If any think they are religious, and do not bridle their tongues, but deceive their hearts, their religion is worthless" (NRSV). James is simply saying that if people don't control their tongues, their religion is useless.

> *"If we don't control our tongues, every part of our life is threatened."*

But in this particular section of chapter 3, he goes even further than that. Always skillful with language and metaphor, he boldly announces that "the tongue is a fire." It has the ability to poison the entire body. And he says that the origin of that fire is hell itself. That's colorful language—but hardly an overstatement.

He uses two more colorful images to talk about the tongue: "bits in a horse's mouth" and "the rudder of a ship." He words it in this way:

> If we put bits into the mouths of horses that they may obey us, we guide their whole bodies. Look at the ships also; though they

are so great and are driven by strong winds, they are guided by a very small rudder wherever the will of the pilot directs.

(James 3:3-4 RSV)

These pictures illustrate two important lessons. First, when we control our tongues, all the rest of our life is under control.

Two, if we don't control our tongues, every part of our life is threatened. The picture that James gives is that of a vast forest set aflame by a very small fire. No wonder James tells us to be "slow to speak."

Somewhere I found someone else's prayer that I have made my own: "Lord, make my words sweet and tender, for I may have to eat them tomorrow."

If we are slow to talk, we will be more likely to fulfill two essentials of integrity and communication.

One, we will say what we mean. How important that is! Since people listen so little, when they do listen to us, it's important that we have said what we mean. Jesus said, "I tell you, on the day of Judgment you will render account for every careless word you utter." And the apostle Paul admonished Timothy, "Avoid godless chatter and contradictions of what is falsely called knowledge." We need to control the tongue, to discipline the tongue by being slow to talk and by saying what we mean.

The only time I ever heard Dr. William Glasser, father of a school of counseling called "reality therapy," he took a page from his family's biography and related how it began. His family home included one of those big bathtubs, and they filled it one evening and asked their five-year-old son if he wouldn't like to get in and splash and play. He did want to, and his parents knew he wanted to, but as five-year-olds sometimes do, he balked and said, "No."

As a matter of fact, he threw a giant-sized fit, screaming and crying that he wanted his own little infant bathtub.

During the howling, his ten-year-old sister said she would like to get into the tub. So she quickly hopped in and proceeded to have a delightful time. With that, the five-year-old changed his tune, demanding to get into the big tub also.

At that point, Dr. Glasser picked up his son, temper and all, took him to the bedroom, undressed him, and put him in his infant tub. He listened to the boy's howls of protest but remained firm.

When the crying subsided, Dr. Glasser said to his son, "After this, never say No when you mean Yes, and never say Yes when you mean No."

As I recall, Dr. Glasser concluded the story with this comment: "Would it not be cruel *not* to teach a child that lesson?"

Of course it would. All of us must learn and relearn that lesson many times. There is too much at stake in our relationships not to say what we mean.

Then there is the second possible outcome of disciplining our tongue and being slow to speak. Not only will we say what we mean, we will mean what we say.

> *"We must say what we mean*
> *and mean what we say."*

There's an old story about a certain bank robber by the name of Jorge Rodriguez who operated along the border at the turn of the century. One day a Texas Ranger saw Rodriguez cross the Rio Grande into Mexico, and he trailed him until they came to a village, where Rodriguez entered a cantina.

The ranger slipped in behind him, put a gun to his head, and said, "I've come to get back all the money you have stolen from the banks in Texas. Unless you tell me where it is, I'm going to shoot you."

Now, Rodriguez could not speak English, and the ranger couldn't speak Spanish. However, a man standing nearby was bilingual, and when he stepped forward and offered to translate, the ranger agreed. So the man explained to Rodriguez that unless he told the ranger where the money was, the ranger would shoot him.

Well, you can imagine how Rodriguez felt, so he answered,

"I've not spent any of the money. Tell the Ranger to go to the well in the center of town, face north, and count five stones down on the inside wall. That stone will be loose, and if he will remove it, he will find all the money behind it. Tell him quickly before he kills me!"

The translator then turned to the Texas Ranger and said, "Jorge Rodriguez is a very brave man. He said he is not afraid to die."

Only our actions prove that we mean what we say. That's why I am always puzzled by people in the church who agree to serve on committees but never show up for a meeting; those who tell you they are going to support and attend an event, but are conspicuous by their absence; those who make a pledge year after year but never honor it.

It is always easier to talk about Jesus than it is to follow him, to discuss love than to share it. It's easier to make promises than it is to keep them.

We can talk a lot about loyalty and honesty and generosity and commitment to Christ—but when decisions must be made and action is called for, it is then that we prove whether we really mean what we say.

Self-respect and trust are at stake here. If people are not given reason to trust us by our daily pattern of living—our fidelity in keeping our word and speaking the truth—why should they trust us when some big issue is at stake?

Vince Lombardi once confronted a star on his championship Green Bay Packers football team and told him, "I saw you cheat on the field today, and I tell you, I won't have it. If you cheat on the field, you will cheat in life."

Listen to James in verses 10, 11, and 12 of chapter 3: "From the same mouth come blessing and cursing. My brethren, this ought not to be so. Does a spring pour forth from the same opening fresh water and brackish? Can a fig tree, my brethren, yield olives, or a grapevine figs? No more can salt water yield fresh" (RSV).

A very clear picture. Our actions determine whether we mean what we say.

David Halberstam, the famous journalist, tells of a friend who was visiting Japan. Reminded that taxi drivers often did not speak English, and that it was a good idea to carry with him something bearing the imprint of his hotel in Japanese, the friend had picked up a small box of matches bearing the name and address of his hotel.

Later, when he had finished his tour of the city, he climbed into a taxi and produced the box of matches for the driver, animatedly pointing to the address of his hotel. The driver's face lit up as if he had just understood, and he quickly sped away. Half an hour later, he brought the car to a screeching halt, turned and beamed at his passenger, and pointed out the window. It was not the hotel, but a match factory!

He had not noticed the address on the box, but he knew what was in the box—matches.

Communication isn't easy, even under the best of circumstances—so we need to be intentional. One, we need to say what we mean and say it clearly. And two, we need to mean what we say.

CHAPTER SEVEN

> *My beloved brothers and sisters, do you with your acts of favoritism really believe in our glorious Lord Jesus Christ? . . . If you show partiality, you commit sin and are convicted by the law as transgressors. (James 2:1, 9 NRSV)*

It Isn't Easy Being Green

Do you remember "It's Not Easy Being Green," the song from "Sesame Street"? I was reminded of this song because of an article written some years ago by a Dr. Ridenour. Dr. Ridenour was a stroke victim. She was a woman in her forties, partially paralyzed, seeking to face the truth of her crippled body. She said it was the most difficult thing she ever had to do. The paralysis was an embarrassment, creating a kind of vulnerability and nakedness, a sadness, and an infinite kind of loneliness.

At the end of the article, she talked about "It's Not Easy Being Green," written to help children recognize racial prejudice and deal with it. Dr. Ridenour said she thought of this song often as she reentered the world after her stroke, because she was totally unprepared for the prejudice (both real and imagined) she encountered. The rejection by family, friends, and strangers was difficult to handle.

She struggled to conquer the feeling of being a freak (green, in a black and white world): "I was fortunate in that my family helped me maintain my sense of humor so that I could laugh or cry and step out to try again. But no, it isn't easy being green."

In this section of his Epistle (2:1-13), James is talking primarily about the sins of prejudice and partiality.

I deliberately began with a stroke-victim's testimony to make real the universality of prejudice. On hearing the scripture, you might have expected me to talk about showing partiality to whites over blacks, or rich over poor; but prejudice runs an almost limitless gamut, according to who we are and where we are. Males over females, young over old, educated over uneducated, urban over rural, Methodist over Pentecostal, Episcopalian over Baptist, Protestant over Catholic, the urbane over the country bumpkin, the sophisticated over the simple—prejudice and partiality are universal. One fellow said, "I look down my nose at people who look down their noses."

James is talking about this universal sin. To be sure, he sets it in the context of wealth, underscoring again that God has taken a preferential option on behalf of he poor. Notice verse 5: "Has not God chosen the poor in the world to be rich in faith and to be heirs of the kingdom that he has promised to those who love him?" (NRSV).

Let this truth burn in your mind: In looking down on the poor, we insult their humanity.

James's opening words seem rather innocent, quite acceptable to most religious folks: "My brothers and sisters, do you with your acts of favoritism really believe in our glorious Lord Jesus Christ?"

James is saying that, as Christians, we are not to be partial, or snobbish, or make any kind of distinction between classes or groups of people, or between individuals.

But when we really dig into his meaning, we see that he is not dealing in innocuous generalities. Instead, he "goes for the jugular" as he paints a rather common and familiar picture (2:2-4). The setting is church. Two visitors arrive at different times.

The first visitor is meticulously dressed in beautifully cut clothes and exudes confidence and self-esteem. This visitor is graciously welcomed and made to feel at home by everyone. The second visitor is quite uncoordinated, looks rumpled and unpressed, is wearing scuffed shoes, appears to be shy and timid, and when he does speak, his conversation is uncouth. This person is ignored and left to sit by himself.

Could it be that James had viewed just such a scene in the synagogue, or in one of those first-century house-churches? Have you ever found yourself in such an uncomfortable situation?

But now the writer speaks directly to his readers: "Listen, my beloved brothers and sisters. Has not God chosen the poor in the world to be rich in faith and to be heirs of the kingdom that he has promised to those who love him?"

Do you see the connection, the amazing similarity between this word of James and Mary's Magnificat—Mary's song as she reflected on the gift God had given her in becoming the mother of Jesus?:

"He has shown strength with his arm; he has scattered the proud in the thoughts of their hearts. He has brought down the powerful from their thrones, and lifted up the lowly; he has filled the hungry with good things, and sent the rich away empty" (Luke 1:51-53 NRSV).

> *"When we dishonor the poor,
> we are dishonoring God."*

In this word, James reveals himself as a New Testament version of an Old Testament prophet. Those spiritual giants were social critics. They were God's instruments to challenge the ways the people related to one another in every part of life. James identifies with the poor and the suffering because they have been exploited by the social structure of the time. He is outraged by the first-century social injustices and says that such practices are completely unacceptable to a loving and compassionate God.

James is telling us that giving any preference to the rich over the poor is evil—that to show partiality to someone because of what he or she possesses is a sin against God. Showing partiality is not Christian and is an offense to a loving Lord who shows partiality to no one. And then James goes even further in these verses, insisting that God has chosen the poor of the world to be rich in the faith—when we dishonor the poor, we are dishonoring God.

Now we begin to understand that the seemingly harmless words that opened our Scripture for this lesson—show no partiality, don't have favorites—are really very powerful. James is writing a prophetic broadside against the evil of valuing persons on the basis of what they have or own. But of even greater significance is his prophetic outcry against the evil distortions in human society between the opportunities available to the rich and those available to the poor.

It was true in the first century, and it is equally true today, that in most countries of the world, the distinction between the poor and the rich is dramatic. In the United States, the rich and the poor are minorities at either end of the spectrum, with a large middle class making up the majority. In viewing the difference between the haves and the have nots of the world, we find that from a global perspective, we in this country are among the haves. By comparison with the vast majority of people in the Third World countries, we are rich.

A few years ago the InterReligious Foundation for Community Organization produced the following statistics. If the world were a village of 100 people, 70 of those people would be unable to read; only one would have a college education. Approximately 50 would be suffering from malnutrition, and more than 80 would be living in what we would consider substandard housing. Only 6 of the hundred would be Americans, and those 6 would own half of the total income. I'm sure the statistics have not changed. We are rich!

If there ever was a people in the history of the human race who needed to grapple with the idea James is writing about here, it is we Americans. Somehow, we must come to see ourselves not as a privileged few, but as part of the whole human family. And then in verses 6 and 7, James reminds his readers of all time that the majority attitude toward the poor is one of disrespect. In looking down on the poor, we insult their humanity. We sin against them and against God.

The sin of prejudice that expresses itself in partiality is universal. James makes that point against the backdrop of a central Christian understanding—*God is not partial*—a thought that is distinctively Christian: "For judgment will be without mercy to anyone who has shown no mercy; mercy triumphs over judgment" (2:13).

James uses the word *law* in the same way John used the word *commandment* when he wrote, "And this is his commandment, that we should believe in the name of his Son Jesus Christ and love one another, just as he has commanded us" (I John 3:23 NRSV).

Now, the law of liberty or freedom, like love, is not something that can be commanded or legislated. With this in mind, we begin to see the picture James is laying out for us. He speaks of the Commandment, "Thou shalt love thy neighbor as thyself," as the *royal law*—first given by God to Israel as a part of the Levitical law, but now revealed through Jesus Christ, who was himself the living and breathing "Royal Law."

James has said here that the opposite of this royal law of love is the showing of partiality. And the prime example of showing partiality, for James, is the way society, down through history, has discriminated against the poor. Now, over against that, James tells us that the mercy that triumphs over "judgment" is the law of liberty or freedom.

And in line with what Jesus said in the Sermon on the Mount, those who will receive mercy have shown mercy: "Blessed are the merciful, *for they shall obtain mercy*" (Matt. 5:7 RSV, italics mine). What we have here is the law of giving and receiving, as our Lord stated in his prayer: "And forgive us our debts, *as we also have forgiven our debtors* (Matt. 6:12 RSV, italics mine). In other words, there can be no partiality in the giving and receiving—the law of liberty is the law of love and mercy.

> *"There are no favorites and no strangers in the Lord's fellowship of believers."*

Here is a powerful lesson for twentieth-century Christians and today's church. We are prone to measure the worth of people by the car they drive, the house they live in, the clubs they belong to, the labels on their clothes. In both our private and our church lives, we are inclined to show partiality for and establish relationships with only those who are at least moderately successful financially. And either consciously or unconsciously, those reputed to be "big givers" are assigned prominent places on church boards and committees.

Am I being too tough? Think about it. Isn't it sometimes true that our efforts at evangelism and outreach are subtlely geared to attract to our particular fellowship people who can enhance its quality and add prestige to the church's standing in the community? And, even when out of feelings of guilt or obligation, we give money to some relief organization, we think of it as a means of "helping those poor people *out there* who wouldn't be poor if they'd go to work." They are different; they are strangers to us.

James is saying bluntly that if we show partiality by showing preferential treatment toward a person based on financial status, we are guilty of sin. And even though we obey the other laws (2:10-11), we are guilty of breaking the law of love, of liberty.

By both attitude and action, we are to recognize that all people—without exception—stand on common ground at the foot of the cross and outside the empty tomb. There are no favorites and no strangers in the Lord's fellowship of believers.

But the sin is universal, for God is not partial. Now that's a tough truth to grapple with—hard to really buy. Can you handle it? God makes no distinctions. God sends the sun and the rain on the just and the unjust, the good and evil alike. Can you believe that?

In a folder of precious keepsakes, I have a Drew Pearson column titled, "A Rabbi's Kindness Didn't Pay in Mississippi." It was written at Christmastime in 1964. The article begins, "Christmas being the anniversary of a Jew born in Bethlehem nearly two thousand years ago, I write the story of a Jew who lives in Mississippi today. His name is Rabbi David Ben-Ami, of Temple B'Nai Israel in Hattiesburg, and his trials and tribulations began when he befriended ministers of other faiths and incurred the wrath of modern money changers."

Pearson goes on to tell about Rabbi Ben-Ami visiting clergymen who had been thrown in jail for demonstrating against racial prejudice; befriending a white Presbyterian minister who had been involved in the struggle for racial justice; assisting in distributing turkeys to needy Mississippi families of all races, under the Dick Gregory Christmas for Mississippi program.

This was too much for the Rabbi's congregation. They insisted that he leave. They were not ruthless, as were the money changers of Jerusalem with another Jew nearly two thousand years ago. They were polite and sympathetic—but they pointed out that they had heavy investments in Hattiesburg, which could be bankrupted by boycotts. Since the Rabbi had no investment in Mississippi, it seemed simpler for him to look for another synagogue.

That clipping is meaningful to me because of an incident that occurred at Christmastime in 1963. We had two children then. With them, my wife and I were driving from Gulfport, Mississippi, to Richton, my parents' home, about one hundred miles away. We had left Gulfport following a church meeting where angry feelings had been expressed about the racial situation and my involvement in it.

It was an unusually cold night. It was sleeting and the road was icy. It was close to midnight out on a dark, lonely highway, when our car stalled. There was little traffic. The children were getting colder and we were getting anxious. After what seemed to be an endless time and the passing of numerous cars, we were almost at the point of desperation when an old model car came to a screeching halt beside us.

I told the driver our plight, and without asking any further questions, he invited us into his car, helped us transfer luggage, and went out of his way to take us to a friend's home in the nearest town, where we could spend the night and attend to the car problem the next day.

This man had an accent different from mine, and I knew he was not a Mississippian. I surmised, as we often wrongly do, that he was Jewish, and his warm ministry of love reminded me of another Jew and a story he had told about a good Samaritan. Before we reached our destination, I learned that I was right. He was Jewish. His name was David Ben-Ami, Rabbi of Temple B'Nai Israel in Hattiesburg.

It was this man that Drew Pearson wrote about a year later. Not only to the disinherited and dejected of the black race, but to a desperate white Anglo-Saxon Protestant Christian minister and his freezing family, this man expressed love. I don't know where Rabbi Ben-Ami is today, but wherever he is, I have a notion he is living in the way of hospitality and mercy that might put most of us Christians to shame.

He has experienced values that transcend religion or race, social or economic boundaries. His synagogue in Hattiesburg may have rejected his witness, but they couldn't annul it. Mississippi and the world is different today from the way it was in 1964. And it will be different tomorrow, because of people like Rabbi David Ben-Ami.

That's what James is talking about: "My brethren, show no partiality as you hold the faith of our Lord Jesus Christ, the Lord of glory" (2:1 RSV).

Though it isn't easy being green, we will live in a way that will enable others to live in their differences, knowing that they are acceptable to God and to us.

CHAPTER EIGHT

> *What good is it, my brothers and sisters, if you say you have faith but do not have works? Can faith save you? . . . So faith by itself, if it has no works, is dead. (James 2:14, 17 NRSV)*

Faith Working in Love

An article by Claire Safran that appeared in *The Reader's Digest* some time ago moved me deeply. It is the story of seventy-nine-year-old Clara Hale and the drug-addicted infants she cares for in a brownstone in Harlem.

In an old bentwood rocker, she soothes a hurting child.

"I love you and God loves you," she promises. "Your mother loves you too, but she's sick right now, like you are." She coaxes the baby to nurse at a bottle. She bathes the child, croons softly, tries a little patty-cake game.

"After a while, maybe you get a smile," she tells a visitor. "So you know the baby's trying too. You keep loving it—and you wait."

The title of this moving story is "Mama Hale and Her Little Angels." It tells of Clara Hale, who has spent a lifetime caring for other women's children. In a fifth-floor walkup, she raised forty foster children as well as three of her own. And now she operates a place called Hale House, a unique haven in the heart of the drug darkness of New York. At the time the article was written, she had cared for 487 babies of addicts. Since then, there have been hundreds more.

Mama Hale would understand what James talked about—"Faith Working in Love"—a description of practical Christianity. She puts it into practice.

I like what Dr. Hans Kung, the brilliant Roman Catholic theologian from Tübingen, Germany, said: "Whoever preaches one-half of the gospel is no less a heretic than the person who preaches the other half of the gospel."

That's the temptation of every preacher—to preach one-half of the gospel. That's the tight-rope we walk, preaching a gospel either of faith alone, or of works alone. James is an unequivocal champion of works. He minces no words. Hear him in these verses:

> What good is it, my brothers and sisters, if you say you have faith but do not have works? Can faith save you? If a brother or sister is naked and lacks daily food, and one of you says to them, "Go in peace; keep warm and eat your fill," and yet you do not supply their bodily needs, what is the good of that? So faith by itself, if it has no works, is dead. (2:14-17 NRSV)

This is the primary emphasis of James's entire Epistle. We must be doers of the word and not hearers only. This is what has caused so many problems for the Epistle through the years. This is the reason Luther called it a "right strawy epistle." Luther was calling his church back to the core of the gospel: Justification by grace through faith. "Faith alone" was his battle cry, and he felt that James was undercutting that core of the gospel by contending that salvation also had to do with works.

So the battle has raged ever since. It reached a current high pitch with the publication of John McArthur's book *The Gospel According to Jesus*. McArthur takes on the big boys like Charles Ryrie, author of the Ryrie Study Bible; two or three other professors at Dallas Theological Seminary; and a number of other well-known theologians in the evangelical world. The current battle swirls around a concept called "Lordship salvation," in conflict with a "belief only" position.

Basically, those who hold the "Lordship salvation" position contend that Jesus doesn't come to us as Savior, offering us eternal salvation, and then come to us later as Lord, with a call to surrender ourselves to him, clean up our lives, and follow him as disciples. He comes to us at one and the same time as Savior and as Lord. To be saved requires that we surrender to Christ as Lord and thus are regenerated by his grace. Now, I agree with that much of the thesis—but not with the *extreme* to which McArthur takes it.

At the other extreme—or the other half of the gospel—is the "belief only" position. It claims that one can be a Christian without being a follower of the Lord Jesus Christ. Does that sound strange? It does when you say it, doesn't it? As strange as it sounds—and though you may not have heard it expressed precisely that way—that is the position of a large wing of evangelical Christianity, represented by such outstanding persons as Ryrie.

Those people are so committed to preserving the gospel of "faith alone" that they separate the offices of Christ. They say that Christ comes to the sinner only as Savior and makes no claims of Lordship, that it is only after we become Christian that the Lordship of Christ has any claim on our life. The bottom line of that belief is that it encourages people to claim Jesus as Savior by simple intellectual affirmation—by saying yes in our mind to "four spiritual laws," or a belief plan of salvation, and defer until later, or never, the claims of Christ in the transformation of life. This leads people to believe that their behavior has no relationship to their spiritual status.

> *"Do you think we would be in the mess we are in if one-third of us was really Christian?"*

Thus there would be nothing uniquely different between Christians, in terms of the way they live their lives in the world, and those who are not Christian. One-third of our nation's population claims to be "born again." Think of that. One-third of the population! Do you think our nation could be drowning in drugs, wallowing in pornography, allowing millions to go hungry and without shelter, cheering self-serving government officials into cutting welfare in order to balance a budget that has been unbalanced for years because it gave more attention to the rich than to the poor—do you think we would be in the mess we are in if one-third of us was really Christian and would listen to Jesus?

"If a brother or sister is naked and lacks daily food, and one of you says to them, 'Go in peace; keep warm and eat your fill,' and yet you do not supply their bodily needs, what is the good of that? So faith by itself, if it has no works, is dead."

Aren't we mocking the gospel when we reduce its requirements to simply believing that Christ dies for our sins—and all he requires of us is to give intellectual assent to that and accept by faith the eternal security he offers?

With that long, long introduction, let's focus on James's teaching.

As you look closely at this word of James, you realize that he is not asking whether *works without faith can save us*. But rather, whether *faith* without works can save us. His answer to that is a resounding No.

Before we take issue with James, see the similarity between his words in our text, verses 14-17, and Jesus' parable of the Last Judgment in Matthew 25. This is the only time Jesus told us what judgment is going to be like. Do you remember the parable? When the Son of Man comes in his glory and gathers before him all the nations of the world, he will separate the sheep from the goats. He will place the sheep at his right hand and the goats at his left. He will say to those on his right hand—the sheep:

> Come, O blessed of my Father, inherit the kingdom prepared for you from the foundation of the world; for I was hungry and you gave me food, I was thirsty and you gave me drink, I was a stranger and you welcomed me, I was naked and you clothed me, I was sick and you visited me, I was in prison and you came to me.
>
> (25:34*b*-36 RSV)

67

That was a surprise to both the righteous and the unrighteous, because neither knew when they had done that sort of thing for Jesus.

"When," they asked, "when did we see you hungry?"

His response to their question is unforgettable: "As you did it [or did it not] to one of the least of these my brethren, you did it [or did it not] to me" (25:40 RSV).

Nothing about belief—nothing about right doctrine—nothing about proper churchmanship.

I think of Linus and his sister, Lucy, in Charles Shultz's "Peanuts" comic.

Linus says to Lucy, "You think you are smart just because you are older than I am!"

Lucy gets up and walks off, but Linus follows, saying, "You just happened to be born first! You were just lucky!" Then he screams, "I didn't ask to be born second." And in the final frame, he adds in despair, "I didn't even get a chance to fill out an application."

When it comes to the Last Judgment, there are no applications to fill out—the conditions have been predetermined by Jesus himself. Think of James in light of that.

So, James's question is not whether works without faith can save us, but whether faith without works can save. So, let's press for clarity by putting the issue into some affirmations.

One, there is no salvation without discipleship. What do I mean by that? I mean that we can't claim Jesus as Savior without a willingness to surrender to him as Lord.

> *"Ethics and good works do not save us, but rather are the expression of the transforming work of the Spirit within us."*

Two, an *emphasis on faith that does not include fidelity to Christ's call to walk in newness of life is a distortion of the gospel.* What do I mean by that? I mean the same thing James was saying in our scripture lesson. I mean that the kind of faith that does not give attention to ethical issues—to telling the truth, seeking to live morally clean lives, shunning evil, fighting personal immorality and social injustice, feeding the hungry, caring for the needy, seeking the lost, suffering for those the world has said no to—that kind of faith, a faith that does not give attention to ethical issues—is dead.

Three, a faith that emphasizes ethics and good works as a saving way of life is a false faith. Does that sound contradictory to what I have been saying? What do I mean? I mean that ethics and good works do not save us, but rather are the expression of the transforming work of the Spirit within us.

That brings us to another point. As good a definition of practical Christianity as you will find comes from Paul. It is this: Faith working in love.

That comes from Galatians: "For in Christ Jesus neither circumcision nor uncircumcision is of any avail, but faith working through love" (5:6 RSV).

Phillips translates it this way: "Faith which expresses itself in love." The New English Bible says: "Faith active in love." Paul is saying that when God comes to judge us, the question is not going to be whether we were obedient to the law, or whether we are circumcised or uncircumcised. The question is going to be whether, in the revelation of God's love expressed ultimately in his crucified Son, we have turned to him in faith. And when there is a testing of that faith, it will involve not the doctrinal positions to which we have given intellectual ascent, but whether our faith expressed itself in love.

So I use Paul's word as a graphic description of what James is calling for: Faith working in love—a good definition of practical Christianity.

Going back to Mama Hale, "The ones who worry her most are the toddlers who arrive scruffy and neglected."

Against the disorder of the world they will return to someday, she teaches them a sense of order. Regular meals and bedtimes. A clean house and clothes.

"Be honest," Mama says. "Be smart," she urges. Lulling a six-month-old baby to sleep, she croons, "One day, when you go to college . . . "

"They don't always know what I'm saying," she says, "but they know I love them." That is part of her "gift," as she calls it, her secret for saving children and changing their lives.

On her bedroom door is the second half of her message, a small sign that says: "You can make it."

Well, they can—and we can—when faith works in love.

CHAPTER NINE

> *Draw near to God, and he will draw near to you. Cleanse your hands, you sinners, and purify your hearts, you double-minded.*
> *(James 4:8 NRSV)*

Draw Near to God

An older couple was motoring down the road on Sunday afternoon. He was driving; she was leaning against the door on her side. They were eager to get where they were going, but had caught up with a slow-moving car ahead of them. The driver was a young man; a young woman cuddled very close to him, almost sitting in his lap, rubbing his face, and now and then kissing him on the cheek. Even though it was dangerous, he would turn around now and then and kiss her. They were in no hurry at all—that is, in no hurry as far as moving the car along.

It was impossible to pass, so the older couple began to talk. The woman looked across at her husband, then looked ahead to the young couple and asked, "Why don't we sit together like that anymore?"

Quick as a flash, he responded, "I haven't moved."

That story stimulates all sorts of suggestive thoughts. Relationships may grow cold over the years. There may be someone you love—husband, wife, child, parent—someone with whom your relationship has grown cold. You may be to blame. The other person may be. In either case, you can do something about it.

Then there's our relationship with God, and that's the point of telling the story. At the heart of this challenging, probing section from James's Epistle is a grace-filled truth. It's in verse 8: "Draw near to God, and he will draw near to you." Think of that possibility—not as a one-time event, but as a life-style—a daily experience: Draw near to God.

Before we focus our thoughts completely on that point, we can't ignore some other powerful truths expressed in this passage of scripture. As with the rest of the Epistle, in almost staccato fashion, James lays it out—bang, bang, bang. And not always are the themes or the thoughts connected. Let's take a brief look at some of them.

First, you are what you desire with a passion, and what you desire with a passion has far-reaching effects.

We sometimes try to excuse ourselves from responsibility by saying, "It's my business—what should it matter to others?" James is dramatic in making his case:

> These conflicts and disputes among you, where do they come from? Do they not come from your cravings that are at war within you? You want something and do not have it; so you commit murder. And you covet something and cannot obtain it; so you engage in disputes and conflicts. You do not have, because you do not ask.
>
> (4:1-2 NRSV)

Wow! Overstated? Maybe. But look at history. What lay behind the spread of the Roman Empire—and its fall? It was the passions of the Emperor. What about the Napoleonic Conquest? Was it not the monstrous ego of "the little general"? The Third Reich and the awful Holocaust?—a result of Hitler's maniacal passion, his lust for power, and his hatred of Jews. Some of the biggest factors in the Middle East crisis that climaxed in the Desert Storm of 1991 were undisciplined greed and the mad passions of a political leader.

It continues to be so. There is a connection between the haves, indulging their wild appetites, and the have-nots, continuing in the chains of poverty. There is a connection between our unwillingness to live simpler lives and our threatened environment.

What is the cause of the massive waste and a drug-dependent

culture that threatens the ruin of our nation? Studies are showing that the fault does not lie in the crime-infested ghettos
alone. That is not where the money is coming from to keep the
drug industry alive. It is the indulgence of the middle- and
upper-middle-class folks who are not willing to discipline their
own appetites, even though the fallout is killing little children
and bringing heroin-addicted babies into the world.

Look at our prison system. Isn't it a failure because we base our
approach to crime upon our passion for vengeance and punishment? We lose the fact that we should be in the business of reha-
bilitation and redemption, not vengeance and punishment.

Look in another direction. What is the primary cause of
divorce that leaves children threatened? Is it not individual selfishness and undisciplined passion?

No mother or father can say to me, "What I do doesn't matter." I've seen too many children, now age 18, 20, even 30 and
40, who are still suffering for the sins of their parents.

So register the truth that James would teach us: You are what
you desire with a passion, and what you desire with a passion has
far-reaching effects.

Now, a second point. You can't be friends of the world and
friends with God at the same time. That's what James says: "Do
you not know that friendship with the world is enmity with God?
Therefore whoever wishes to be a friend of the world becomes
an enemy of God" (4:4 NRSV).

Remember now, James and other biblical writers use "the
world" as a symbol for those priorities and values that oppose
and are at war with God's fellowship of believers, his new society.

James, and Paul especially, use the terms *flesh* and *world* to
refer to the evil power around us that opposes God and drives us
to want things that others have, to even be willing to fight and
wage war to get them. That's the reason James puts it so bluntly:
"Whoever wishes to be a friend of the world becomes an enemy
of God."

It's also why he has told us to be unstained or unspotted by
the world. We can't be friends of God, at peace with God,
accepted by God, and at the same time be comfortable with the
evil influence of the world around us. It is the world that creates

havoc in every part of our life. It is the influence of the world—
the lust for power, the passion for control, the desire to do as we
please, the insistence that things be done our way—that creates
strife and plays havoc in our life and in our relationships.

> *"Never play leapfrog with a unicorn."*

There's a beautiful phrase in verse 5: "God yearns jealously for
the spirit that he has made to dwell in us" (4:5*b* NRSV). James is
remembering the first of the Ten Commandments: "You shall
have no other gods before me" (Exod. 20:3); and he is also
recalling that phrase in the second Commandment: "For I the
Lord your God am a jealous God" (Exod. 20:5*b*).

You can't be friends of the world and friends of God at the
same time. Someone has put it graphically: "Never play leapfrog
with a unicorn."

Do you need to stop for a moment and let the incisive wisdom
of that warning sink in? Picture the unicorn, a deer-like creature
that has one single sharp horn protruding from the center of its
head. It's not difficult to see the dangers of playing leapfrog with
such a creature.

I got that image from the little book *Keep It Simple: Daily Medita-
tions for Twelve-Step Beginnings and Renewal,* which elaborates on
the Alcoholics Anonymous program. In comparing that program
to our relationship with God, we realize that this is what James is
saying—that we know our limits and accept them—and it's true
in every area of life. We can't play leapfrog with a unicorn. We
can't be friends of God and friends of the world at the same time.

James makes the point that such a compromising life-style—
seeking to be friends of God and friends of the world at the
same time—even plays havoc with our prayer life: "You ask and
do not receive, because you ask wrongly, in order to spend what
you get on your pleasures" (4:3 NRSV).

The point James is making here is that when we are not right
with God—when our friendship with him is blurred because of

our friendship with the world—we either don't ask him for what we need, or we ask him for the right things, but with the wrong purpose and motive. We pray for good things with the intention of using them for our own gain and selfish pleasure.

Someone told me a story about a man who was boasting to an evangelist about the fact that God had given him a new Cadillac: "I prayed to the Lord, and I gave Him 10 percent of my income, and he blessed me with a new Cadillac."

"Is that right," the evangelist exclaimed.

"Oh yes, sir," the man responded. "I gave the Lord 10 percent of everything I made and prayed for a new Cadillac, and the Lord came through. Ain't that wonderful?"

The evangelist was very pointed in his response: "That's interesting. You prayed to God, and he gave you a Cadillac. But when his own son prayed to him, God gave him an ugly cross on which to die."

You see, there's something contradictory about seeking to be humble and obedient and, at the same time, praying for a Cadillac. It's one thing to be in need of transportation and pray that your need will be met. It's something else to pray that your transportation need will be met in the form of a BMW. That's playing leapfrog with a unicorn.

The lusts that war within us reduce our prayers to selfishness and cause us to try to use God, rather than giving ourselves to be used by God. So nail it down. You can't be friends with the world and friends with God at the same time.

That brings us to the third point of this passage of James: "Draw near to God, and he will draw near to you."

James gives us rather clear directions for drawing near to God: "Submit yourselves therefore to God. Resist the devil, and he will flee from you. Draw near to God, and he will draw near to you. Cleanse your hands, you sinners, and purify your hearts, you double-minded" (4:7-8 NRSV).

> There are our directions:
> One—We are to submit ourselves to God.
> Two—We are to resist the devil.
> Three—We are to live repentantly.

Let's look briefly at these directions. First, submit to God. Now, that doesn't sound too exciting, does it? We moderns don't even like the word *submit*. It goes against the grain of our macho "take control" stance.

But isn't this attitude the source of most of our problems? We seek to control our own lives, to control our own destiny, to go on our own power—and look where we are.

Again, I turn to the little book, *Keep It Simple*. One of the writers quotes Erma Bombeck, who said, "Never go to a doctor whose office plants have died."

> *"Satan is an active force in the world."*

That's rather suggestive, isn't it? We've tried it our own way. We've followed the way of the world. We've trusted others— we've been to doctors whose office plants have died—and where are we? To draw near to God, we must submit ourselves to God, surrender our lives to God's guidance.

Then the second direction James gives us is to resist the devil. Is your devil too small? Many of us treat the devil as though he were a symbol of evil, rather than an active evil force and an encourager of evil. More and more, I'm convinced that Satan is an active force in the world. When we're honest, most of us will confess that there is something in life that lures us off the right path. We all feel it at one time or another. James is urging us to acknowledge that fact, confess the influence, and by deliberate prayer, resist that power; submit yourself to God and call on Christ to empower you to resist.

Submit to God, resist the devil, and now, the third direction for drawing near to God—live repentantly. "Cleanse your hands," James says, "and purify your hearts." That is living repentantly.

Repentance is more than just acknowledging our sin. It is that, to be sure. But it is also the deep desire to cease our sinful action and be freed of our sinful attitudes and feelings. Someone once put it this way: "To err is human, but when the eraser wears out ahead of the pencil, you're overdoing it."

We must live repentantly in order to live in a stance of drawing near to God. Every time we find ourselves veering off center, moving away from God in attitude or action, we must acknowledge it to ourselves, confess it to God, and allow the Presence of the indwelling Christ to empower us to live rightly. Living repentantly—it's a day-to-day process!

Let's rehearse what we have considered:

One, we are what we desire with a passion, and what we desire with a passion has far-reaching effects.

Two, we can't be friends of the world and friends of God at the same time.

Three, to draw near to God as an ongoing style, we must:

1. Submit ourselves to God;
2. Resist the devil; and
3. Live repentantly.

It's one of the greatest offers we will ever be given: "Draw near to God, and he will draw near to you." How are you responding to the offer?

CHAPTER TEN

> *What is your life? For you are a mist that appears for a little while and then vanishes. . . . Instead you ought to say, "If the Lord wishes, we will live and do this or that."*
> *(James 4:14b-15 NRSV)*

What Is Your Life?

When historian H. G. Wells died in 1946, many newspapers quoted the last words he ever spoke. Friends and nurses were fluttering about his bedside trying to be helpful, adjusting pillows, pulling up covers, administering sedatives, and so on.

Wells turned to them and said, "Don't bother me. Can't you see I'm busy dying?" It was the last flicker of humor from a gallant spirit.

That story causes us to think about the way people die. The way they die says a lot about the way they have lived; in fact, it says almost everything about the way they lived. And I keep asking myself, "Am I living in such a way that I could share at least a little bit of humor on my deathbed?"

Tony Campolo, that remarkable Christian communicator, tells about the Baptist Church of which he is the associate pastor in Philadelphia. It celebrates Student Recognition Day once a year.

In one of those services, after a few students had spoken, the Pastor stood up and said, "Young people, you may not think you are going to die, but you are. One of these days, they'll take you to the cemetery, drop you in a hole, throw some dirt on your face, and go back to the church and eat potato salad."

What a sermon opener! But what an unforgettable underscoring of the inevitable fact of death.

What might we be doing on our deathbed? What might we be saying? All of us are going to die. We know that. But do we live as though we know it?

In this scripture passage, James emphasizes the truth that a life of faith is one of daily dependence on the Lord. Our day-to-day planning must always be done with the awareness that our minutes, our hours, and our days are subject to the will of the Lord. James describes our life as "a mist that appears for a little while and then vanishes." Then he adds that our attitude at all times must be: "If the Lord wishes, we will live and do this or that" (4:15).

Let's be clear. Those words are not intended to minimize right planning and preparation for each day of our lives, but to stress the overriding importance of living each day in complete dependence on the Lord.

> *"All of us are going to die. We know that. But do we live as though we know it?"*

So in the midst of this passage, James asks the penetrating question, "What is your life?" And he helps us to answer it.

In one of Arthur Miller's plays called *The Price,* a middle-aged couple are reminiscing. Life had turned out to be a disappointment. They thought they had it all mapped out. They knew what they wanted to do, the academic degrees they needed. Their goals had seemed clear. But they never realized those goals.

At a climactic moment of the play, the woman says to her husband, "Everything was always temporary with us. It's as if we never were anything. We were always just about to be."

Isn't that tragic? But it's not an uncommon experience. Many of us enter middle age and look down the road toward a retirement that is not far away, and we wonder what happened. Where did it all go? Where did we make the wrong turn? Or maybe we didn't make a wrong turn—maybe we didn't make a turn at all. Or maybe, at a crucial moment, we failed to decide. We were too afraid to take the risk. So we stand, asking the question that was asked in the song—"Is That All There Is?"

Well, it doesn't matter where we are in life or how old we are, the question is always appropriate: "What is your life?"

Implicit in our scripture lesson is James' answer—"Life is gift." Also implicit is a second answer—"Life is opportunity."

Before we look at those two understandings of life, let's make the point that the way we look at life makes all the difference in the world.

John Claypool recalls a story told by Alfred Adler—an intriguing encounter that took place in the main train station of inner Austria, back in the early 1930s.

A well-dressed businessman got off the train and was walking through the lobby, when an alcoholic beggar stopped him and asked for just enough money for one more meal. The businessman said he did not usually respond to such requests, but he would on one condition.

He said, "Tell me, how has an intelligent-looking person, as you appear to be, allowed yourself to get into these straits?"

With that, the beggar turned red in the face with anger and responded, "Listen, if you had happen to you what has happened to me, you wouldn't be asking that question. You would be exactly where I am. . . . I was one of several children. My mother died when I was young. My father was an abusive and very cruel man. The state finally took my brothers and sisters and me away from him and put us in an orphanage. During World War I, a battle raged around our orphanage, the building caught fire, and I had to flee into the night. I have never seen any of my family since. I don't know whether they are alive or dead. It's been that way all my life. Every time I try to get on my feet, something knocks me down. If you had happen to you what's happened to me, you would be standing in these very shoes."

The businessman said, "It's interesting you should say that, because as you tell your story, it does, in fact, parallel my own." Shocked that their stories were so related, they began to talk more fully. As you probably have anticipated, they discovered that they were in fact brothers, separated years before and now, mysteriously, their lives again had intersected.

Dr. Adler used this story to raise the perplexing question, "Why is it that we humans respond so differently to the same circumstances?" Here were two individuals who had the same genetic background, who had much the same things happen to them, and yet, while one had allowed those events to crush him to the ground, the other, like a sail tacking into the wind, had somehow used things that might go against him as energy to move forward. Why did these two brothers respond so differently to the same set of circumstances?

George Buttrick gets at the same question with a different metaphor: "Why is it, do you suppose, that the same sun melts the wax and hardens the clay?" Or Oscar Wilde's couplet: "Two men looked through the selfsame bars: One saw mud, the other stars." Two people look on exactly the same landscape; one pair of eyes gravitates to the lowest and the grimiest; the other pair, for some reason, reaches up to the highest and the best. Why is it that we respond so differently to the same set of circumstances?

So how we look at life makes all the difference in the world. With that as a foundation thought, let's focus now on Life as Gift and Life as Opportunity.

> *"If you feel that life is gift, not entitlement, you can move through life with a kind of lightness."*

Geddes MacGregor tells that when he was six years old, he went with his mother to visit her mother, his grandmother. One afternoon, the grandmother said offhandedly to his mother, "I'm so glad you decided to have little Geddes, because he's been such a pleasure to all of us."

Geddes suddenly appeared and asked, "What do you mean, Grandmother?"

He learned that his mother, who had been forty-eight when he was conceived, had considered having a therapeutic abortion to protect her life. At the last moment, she had decided to go ahead and risk the pregnancy.

Geddes said that he went off to assimilate this new information, and as he sat alone, there came to his precocious childhood fantasy two very vivid images.

In the first image, he saw himself in a line of people walking step by step up to a big portal. Suddenly a hand reached out, pulled him from the line, and said, "You've been disqualified. You cannot be born."

Then that image dissolved and a new image appeared. Again he was in a line, and again moving toward the door. Only this time, he made it through and was born.

Geddes MacGregor said that from that day forward, he has never taken his life for granted for a single moment. Realizing how close he came to not being has made the wonder of aliveness the astonishingly gracious gift that it really is.

Do you see your life as gift? Or like so many, do you see it as some sort of entitlement—something you deserve, or must do? It makes all the difference in the world in the way you view life.

If you see life as an entitlement—something you deserve, or something you must accomplish—then there will be all sorts of pressures: pressure to perform; pressure to be worthy; pressure to be accepted by others; pressure to make things happen; pressure to stand up under the burden that comes from thinking that everything rests on your shoulders.

But if you feel that life is gift, not entitlement, then you can move through life with a kind of lightness. A sense of wonder will pervade your being, and the theme song of your life will be one of gratitude.

Life is gift. And as gift, it is opportunity.

Roy L. Smith, an exciting Methodist preacher of another generation, once told his congregation about the day he watched his five-year-old boy head off to kindergarten. He looked at the proud little fellow, scrubbed, starched, and probably looking better than he ever would look again until he went to his senior prom.

He had a little box of pencils in his hand and a smile on his face. The sun was shining as if it couldn't contain itself.

The little boy turned around to wave at his mother and daddy one more time.

"And he never returned," Dr. Smith said. "He never returned."

No, the boy wasn't killed or kidnapped. He came home at noontime. But he wasn't the same boy anymore. And he never again would be. He had launched into the sea of a new life.

And that's a picture of life. Life is opportunity, an opportunity to be faithful, to be good stewards of the gift that God has given us.

A teacher once had her class conduct an experiment with "jumping" fleas. The students put hundreds of fleas on a table and observed how they jumped. Then they took a large glass container and turned it upside down over the fleas. Now when the fleas jumped, they kept hitting the top of the container. When finally they realized they couldn't jump any higher, they began to measure their jumps.

Later, the teacher removed the container. But the fleas continued to jump at the same height, as if the container were still overhead.

That's a parable of life. Too easily, we allow circumstances to limit us. We settle for less than is possible. We allow mediocrity to become the mean, the standard of our life. So we are not faithful—we are not good stewards of the gift God has given us.

This is glaringly illustrated in our stewardship of financial resources. Scores of people in the congregation I serve have been giving $100 a month to the church for the past five years. They never question their stewardship. Are they being faithful? Since their circumstances have changed—they are now earning far more—should they reassess their giving? And other scores of people settle in at other levels.

The point is, too many of us settle in. We never consider the blessings God has bestowed upon us. We give no thought to the opportunity of apportionment giving, or tithing. We don't think how easy it would be to give an additional $10 or $25 a week. We miss the joy of giving and the meaning of Christian stewardship.

A friend sent me a cartoon recently. It pictures a preacher in a pulpit high above the sanctuary, looking out over his congregation and holding a lottery ticket in his hand.

He says to the congregation, "We appreciate the parishioner who puts a lottery ticket in the collection plate each week. We would appreciate it even more if he would do it before the winners were announced."

Life is gift, and as gift, it is opportunity. It is opportunity for faithfulness, opportunity to express our stewardship for God's gifts.

I came across a marvelous verse of scripture recently that I had never noted before. Does that happen to you now and then? You've read the passage countless times, but suddenly something happens. A light goes on in your mind; your heart stands at attention as you read a word that never before had registered. It was in Chapter 9 of II Corinthians. I was reading the New English Bible, and this is what verse 10 says: "Now he who provides seed for sowing and bread for food will provide the seed for you to sow; he will multiply it and swell the harvest of your benevolence, and you will always be rich enough to be generous."

Wow! Does it hit you as it did me?—"Rich enough to be generous"!

Oh, to be rich in that way—and any one of us can be. That has nothing to do with how much we earn, or how much we have—we all can be rich enough to be generous. And we will be, when we see life as opportunity—opportunity to be faithful, opportunity to practice our stewardship.

Then this final word—when we know that life is opportunity, we will know it as opportunity for commitment.

CHAPTER ELEVEN

> *Be patient, therefore, beloved, until the coming of the Lord. The farmer waits for the precious crop from the earth, being patient with it until it receives the early and the late rains. You also must be patient. Strengthen your hearts, for the coming of the Lord is near.*
> *(James 5:7-8 NRSV)*

Pack Up Your Troubles

In 1942, a man named Felix Powell sat down at a piano to play an old tune. He had every right to play it; he had written it himself. It had been tremendously popular in both World Wars. He was singing it now:

"So pack up your troubles in your old kit bag,
and smile, smile, smile."

When Felix Powell finished his song, he walked into his bedroom, took out a revolver, put it to his head, and shot himself. He could write a song about not worrying, and about smiling, but he was unable to save himself.

It's a sad story, but the message of the song is on target. There is a way to pack up our troubles.

In a cartoon, "Ziggy" has his nightcap and nightshirt on, has closed the front door, and obviously is going to bed. He says,

"My philosophy is, leave your worries on your doorstep—and somebody will probably swipe them!"

Well, that's not the answer. That's not the way to pack up our troubles. But James (5:1-11) helps us with an answer. Now, you may not think so if you stay too long with the first verses of chapter 5. In colorful language, James lashes out at the first-century Jewish Christians who were hoarding their money and failing to care for the less fortunate—the have-nots. The litany is scathing:

Misery is coming—weep and howl.

Your money and material goods are falling apart.

Your clothes are motheaten.

Your gold and silver is rusted and will eat into your being.

You have stored up goods for the future; you have robbed your workers of their wages.

These first six verses do not present a pretty picture. But in verse 7, James begins to talk about the coming of the Lord. I think there are three guiding principles here—three directions that will enable us to pack up our troubles and live joyfully and with meaning, no matter what our circumstances:

One, don't let yesterday rob you of tomorrow.

Two, tend to unfinished business now. Live today as though it were your last.

And three, know that the uncertain future has a certain hope for the Christian.

When we look at the first principle—don't let yesterday rob you of tomorrow—we see that James is focusing on the future. Even so, he does not deny the past. And register this in a special way: James does not offer any hope that we will not suffer the consequences of our past. He makes that rather clear in verse 1: "Come now, you rich people, weep and wail for the miseries that are coming to you" (NRSV). So there are consequences of what we have done, how we have lived, and we don't escape those consequences.

I came across a marvelous expression of this in my devotional Bible reading recently—Romans 6:21. I was reading from the Revised Standard Version, and this is what that translation says: "But then what return did you get from the things of which you are now ashamed? The end of those things is death."

I did with that verse what I often do with words of scripture that really grab my mind. I read it in other translations, and this was the striking way Phillips put it: "Yet, what sort of harvest did you reap from those things that today you blush to remember? In the long run those things mean one thing only—death."

Isn't that a probing question? What sort of harvest did you reap from those things that today you blush to remember? It's true with all of us, isn't it? There are things in our life—things we have done in the past, relationships, circumstances in which we became involved—all sorts of things that we blush to remember.

And the harvest of those things is certain. There are consequences. And we should blush when we remember our yesterdays' sins and failures. But the gospel is that we don't need to let yesterday rob us of tomorrow.

That folk theologian, Yogi Berra, one of the greats of baseball, put it this way: "It's not over till it's over." Yogi was right. Baseball teaches us that in all sorts of ways. In 1986, for instance, Bob Brenley, catcher for the San Francisco Giants, set a major-league record with *four errors in one game* against the Atlanta Braves.

In that same game, he came up to bat in the ninth inning. The Braves were leading. The count was three balls and two strikes. It was the last inning. Do you know what happened? Bob Brenley, in that game in which he had set a world record for errors, hit a home run and won the game for San Francisco, seven to six.

> "Repentance is the experience that enables us to close the door on yesterday."

You see, it's never over till it's over. In theological circles, we talk about grace. Grace means that we always have another chance. Each of us has the chance to live as though what happened in the past doesn't matter.

Repentance is the experience that enables us to close the door on yesterday, in order that we might open the door on tomorrow. This is true, because as James says in verse 11 *c,* "You have seen the purpose of the Lord, how the Lord is compassionate and merciful."

So that's the first direction. Don't let yesterday rob you of tomorrow.

Now the second: Tend to unfinished business today. Live today as though it were your last.

There's a story that speaks to us here—a story of two priests who experienced a rich and rewarding friendship. They struggled together through the wilderness of long seminary training and worked together in a community ministry. Then one of the two was hit by a car and killed in front of their residence. The other knelt at the side of his old friend, gently cradled the man's head on his arm, and before all the people who had gathered, blurted out, "Don't die! You can't die! I never told you that I loved you."

Most of us have regrets like that—maybe not so dramatic, but real and painful. Now and then when I am visiting with people who have experienced the death of a loved one, they will say things like this: "You know, I could have visited Momma more often than I did," or, "I wish I had shared with Dad the things that were important to me and listened to what was important to him."

A recent word brought me to tears, because the man who shared it was crying: "You know, Dad never liked what I did with my life. He wanted me to be a doctor. I felt he never loved me like he loved my sister. But a few days before his death, for the first time since I finished college, he told me he loved me. We could have been such support for one another."

Our unfinished business may not be that dramatic, but most of us have some, and we need to attend to that business now. We need to live today as though it were our last day.

And now this final word to enable us to pack up our troubles: The uncertain future has a certain hope for Christians.

Look at verses 7 and 8 again: "Be patient, therefore, beloved, until the coming of the Lord. The farmer waits for the precious crop from the earth, being patient with it until it receives the early and the late rains. You also must be patient. Strengthen your hearts, for the coming of the Lord is near."

> *"We can pack up our troubles because we know that the uncertain future has a certain hope."*

In these verses, James emphasizes two truths related to the second coming of Jesus. In verse 7, he promises us that Christians will be rewarded for their faithfulness. And in verse 8, we find the word that the coming of the Lord is not only certain, but that it is *near*. Jesus made it plain to his disciples before his death and before his ascension that he would return. We can count on it: Our Lord will return. And Jesus also said that no one except the Father knew when that would be.

When his disciples pressed Jesus for more information about when he would return, he made it clear that that wasn't for them to know. Their task, and ours, is to work and live and witness to the Good News of Jesus Christ. And he further reassured them, and us, that he would be with us in the person and power of the Holy Spirit. We can pack up our troubles, because we know that the uncertain future holds a certain hope.

Jesus seems not so much to be emphasizing that his second coming is going to be *soon* as that it is going to be *sudden*. Again and again, he urged those who heard him to be ready for his *unexpected* return.

Interestingly, in this passage, James is not trying to shock us or scare us with the fact that the Lord is going to return soon. Rather, he is counseling us to be *patient* until the coming of the Lord.

He uses a familiar image—the farmer waiting patiently, knowing that the rains will come—today, tomorrow, next week—they will come. And when the rains come, the fruit will grow, and the harvest will be sure.

James sounds this note of patience again in verses 10 and 11, holding up the prophets as an example. He specifically mentions Job. As William Barclay notes in the Daily Study Bible:

> We generally speak of the *patience* of Job, and that indeed is the word which the Authorized Version uses. But patience is far too passive a word. There is the sense in which Job was anything but patient. As we read the tremendous drama of his life, we see him passionately resenting what has come upon him, passionately questioning the conventional and orthodox arguments of his so-called friends, passionately agonizing over the terrible thought that God might have forgotten and forsaken him. There are few men who have spoken such passionate words as Job spoke. But the great fact about Job is that in spite of all his torrent of questionings, and in spite of the agonizing questionings which tore at his heart, he never lost his faith in God. . . .
>
> The word used of him is that great New Testament word *hupomone,* the word which describes, not a passive patience, but that gallant spirit which can breast the tides of doubt and sorrow and disaster, and still hold on, and come out with faith still stronger on the other side.

That's what James is talking about: *the confidence that the uncertain future has a certain hope.*

Here it is in the testimony of one who learned it late—but learned it, nonetheless. Michael Schafernocker, from Arlington, Texas, a helicoptor door gunner in Vietnam, met God for the first time as he prepared for battle:

> Look, God, I have never spoken to you,
> but now I want to say, "How do you do."
> You see, God, they told me you didn't exist.
> And like a fool, I believed all this.
>
> Last night from a shell hole I saw your sky.
> I figured right then they had told me a lie.
> Had I taken time to see the things you made,
> I'd have known they weren't calling a spade a spade.
>
> I wonder, God, if you'd take my hand.
> Somehow, I feel you will understand.
> Funny, I had to come to this hellish place

Before I had time to see your face.

Well, I guess there isn't much more to say.
But I'm sure glad, God, I met you today.
I guess the zero hour will soon be here,
But I'm not afraid since I know you are near.

The signal—well, God, I'll have to go.
I like you lots and I want you to know.
Look now, this will be a horrible fight.
Who knows, I may come to your house tonight.

Though I wasn't friendly to you before,
I wonder, God, if you'd wait at the door.
Look, I'm crying. Me, shedding tears!
I wish I'd have known you these many years.

Well, God, I'll have to go now, good-bye;
Strange, since I met you . . . I'm not afraid to die!

Not good poetry, some would say, but it's a powerful witness, a powerful witness to three truths:

One—Don't let yesterday rob you of tomorrow.

Two—Tend to unfinished business now—that is, live today as though it were your last.

Three—Know that the uncertain future has a certain hope for the Christian.

CHAPTER TWELVE

> *If anyone among you wanders from the truth and*
> *is brought back by another, you should know*
> *that whoever brings back a sinner from*
> *wandering will save the sinner's soul from death*
> *and will cover a multitude of sins.*
> *(James 5:19b-20 NRSV)*

Who Are Christians?

ot long ago, when I was returning from a teaching-preaching engagement away from Memphis, I had a layover in Detroit. Airports are not among my favorite places. When I have some time in them, I usually find a quiet place, if one is available, and work.

But this time my mind was too weary for reading or reflecting, so I walked. I began to look intentionally at the travel posters on the walls around each gate area. It's beautiful photography. I paid attention to posters from different cities and countries. Obviously, the art was what whoever designed them wanted you to know about the city or country. It was an invitation—"Come-on, look at us. This is what we are."

The poster for New York City had the mighty, but charming Lady of Liberty imposed over the Manhattan skyline.

The poster for Germany had the Bavarian snowcapped mountains in the distant background, a beautiful tall-steepled village church framed against the mountains.

Las Vegas was bright lights—a huge roulette wheel pervading the poster, a hotel markee in sparkling lights announcing "jackpot."

Puerto Rico pictured the beautiful balcony of a snow-white house with a red-tiled roof, bushes of red geraniums, with palm trees and the ocean spreading out before you.

I thought I was too weary to think, but those posters set me to reflecting. If the Church created a poster to invite folks to visit us, what would we present? Who are we Christians?

There is a sense in which we have been dealing with this question in all these reflections. It is certainly what we see in this last section of James's Epistle (5:13-20). It is James's word portrait of the church, who we are as Christians. If any artist-reader is inclined to create an invitational poster for the church, you'll need to include three dynamics: praying, celebrating, caring. You who are not artists will have to settle for *my* word picture.

First, praying. "Are any among you suffering? They should pray," James says (5:13a NRSV). But not just "should pray."

"Are any among you sick? They should call for the elders of the church, and have them pray over them, anointing them with oil in the name of the Lord. The prayer of faith will save the sick, and the Lord will raise them up; and anyone who has committed sins will be forgiven" (5:14-15 NRSV).

The church is a praying place and a praying people. Prayer is too big a subject to pursue with precision. Here are some broad strokes in my word picture:

Prayer does something *in* us.

Prayer does something *for* us.

Prayer does something *through* us.

James says it again and again: "The prayer of faith will save the sick"; "The prayer of the righteous is powerful and effective" (5:16c NRSV). The church is a praying place and a praying people.

Two, the church is a celebrating place and a celebrating people. James says it: "Are any cheerful? They should sing songs of praise" (5:13b NRSV).

It was characteristic of early Christians that they were always ready to burst into song. The early church was a singing church, and their singing was a sign of the people's joy in the Lord. Their joy was rooted in their confidence in God's salvation, his enabling presence in their lives, and his early return.

93

Jesus had given his early followers this warning and promise: "In the world you face persecution. But take courage; *I have conquered the world!*" (John 16:33*b,c*, NRSV, italics mine). With that kind of assurance, it is no wonder that G. K. Chesterton said that joy "is the gigantic secret of the Christian."

> ## *"The pseudo-joy offered by the world is capricious and limited."*

Brian Bauknight, a minister-colleague, tells that when he and his sisters were quite young, their father used to love to demonstrate his zest for living by jumping into the air, then clicking his heels together before descending. He especially loved to do this at what were deemed inappropriate times. The family would be in some very formal or awesome setting, and he would quietly say, "I feel a jump coming on." Embarrassed, all the children would protest, but he would do it anyway.

Every day, life offers all sorts of reasons for joy and celebration. But most of us don't see them, and even when we see them, we control ourselves. We squelch our emotions; we clench our hands rather than clap; we hold our lips tight, lest we surprise others with a shout of excitement.

I don't know how an artist could picture it for a poster, but Toyota should not be able to outdo us Christians in symbolizing the "jump of joy." The pseudo-joy offered by the world is capricious and limited. It comes and goes by chance. But the joy Jesus gives is not dependent upon circumstances, but on our relationship with Jesus Christ. The church is a celebrating place and a celebrating people.

Three, the church is a caring place and a caring people. Our passage from James is shot through with that dynamic: Are any suffering . . . pray. Are any sick . . . call the elders. . . . Confess your sins to one another, and pray for one another. And note especially this: "My brothers and sisters, if anyone among you wanders from the truth and is brought back by another, you should know that whoever brings back a sinner from wandering will save the sinner's soul from death and will cover a multitude of sins" (5:19-20 NRSV).

The whole passage is a picture of a caring community, people attending to the needs of others. Here's a picture of a more modern version of caring.

There were 155 people on board the plane flying home from Australia on Friday, February 24, 1989. A cargo door failed, and a huge hole was ripped open in the side of the aircraft. Nine persons perished when the pressurized air inside blew them into the thin, rarified air at 24,000 feet.

Kerry Lappan, age 31, sitting by the fateful hole, said to reporters, "The whole plane was falling to pieces, and I thought, 'This is it!' but there was a man in front of me. I don't know who he was—a wonderful, wonderful man. He held my hand, and he comforted me. It was so loving and so comforting to have someone's hand to hold."

And not only when our life is threatened—it's always comforting to have someone's hand to hold . . .

. . . when as a teenager, we lost the love we thought was forever.

. . . when as a parent, our teenage children are trying their wings.

. . . when a spouse has died.

. . . when our job has folded and our bank account is dwindling.

. . . when someone has spoken a harsh word that wounded our heart.

There are all sorts of occasions when it's so comforting to have someone's hand to hold, and the church ought to be that kind of place—where people hold the hands of people in need. And more—where people who care reach out in love and concern to persons outside the church. It's not likely that people who need the saving gospel and the sustaining fellowship that the church has to offer—it's not likely that they'll receive it unless it is given by the hands of genuinely caring folks.

"Jesus was God with skin on his face."

So there it is. James's word picture of the church. I don't know how we would present it on a poster to hang in an airport—A Praying, Celebrating, Caring Place and People. Come to think of it, maybe we don't need a poster in the airport or anyplace else. You be the poster, and I'll be the poster.

A small boy, after being tucked into bed for the night, cried out, "Mommy, I'm afraid to be alone in the dark. I want somebody to stay with me."

His mother responded, "Don't be afraid. God is with you."

The little boy then said sadly, "I want somebody with skin on his face."

Jesus was God with skin on his face. And now, you and I are Christ—"little Christs," if you like—with skin on our faces. So we'll be the posters—the living posters.